THE
VACCINATION
BIBLE

D1427545

Edited by
Lynne McTaggart

A WHAT DOCTORS DON'T TELL YOU PUBLICATION

First published in Great Britain in 2000 by What Doctors Don't Tell You Limited, Satellite House, 2 Salisbury Rd, London SW19 4EZ.

Editor and Co-Publisher Lynne McTaggart; Publisher Bryan Hubbard.

ISBN 0 9534734 0 6

For our children:

Caitlin, Anya, Caleb, Esme, Saul, Alexander, Edward and Sophie

And for all your children

ABOUT WHAT DOCTORS DON'T TELL YOU

What Doctors Don't Tell You, the publisher of The Vaccination Bible, has been telling people about the secrets of orthodox medicine for more than 10 years. Its principal publication is the monthly newsletter of the same name, which was first published in 1989. Today it is read by subscribers in over 100 countries around the world who have come to rely on its in-depth research. The company has also published more than 25 books on specific health issues.

Its sister publication is Proof!, a quarterly newsletter that looks at the scientific evidence for alternative treatments and remedies. The company also publishes a magazine, Natural Parent, which promotes alternative and holistic parenting ideas.

To find out more about What Doctors Don't Tell You and its sister publications, please write to: WDDTY, Satellite House, 2 Salisbury Rd, London SW19 4EZ, Tel: 020 8 944 9555 Fax: 020 8 944 9888, or e-mail: wddty@zoo.co.uk.

~oOo~

What Doctors Don't Tell You's editor is Lynne McTaggart, an award-winning journalist and author who regularly appears on TV and radio, as well as in the national press.

CONTENTS

INTRODUCTION

The most important decision you will ever make about your children is whether or not to have them vaccinated. This book pulls together all the evidence that **What Doctors Don't Tell You** has amassed about childhood vaccinations, as well as adult vaccines for flu, hepatitis B and travel.

Most doctors fervently believe that vaccines are one of medical science's greatest success stories, responsible for wiping out many deadly infectious disease. Our view it is that, with vaccines, most medical people have lost all reason about disease and its prevention. So steadfast is their faith in the rightness of their cause that it prevents doctors from acknowledging clear factual evidence demonstrating dangers or ineffectiveness, or even cases of a disease in children who have been vaccinated against it. It also turns otherwise reasonable doctors or scientists into bullies and hysterics, shouting down dissenters, using emotional blackmail to bully parents into submission and resorting to emotive appeals, rather than common sense or fact, in arguing their point of view.

In this zealous climate, amid the rush to "conquer" every possible disease, in which entire reputations rest on defending vaccination at all costs, no one is pausing to examine the possible long-term effect of pumping nine or more different antigens into the immature immune systems of a generation of babies under 15 months. Counting all multiple boosters in the entire suggested schedule, American children can receive some 30 vaccinations by the time they go to school, most in the first few months of life; Britain, with its tuberculosis vaccine offered at birth, but no hepatitis B or chickenpox vaccine, ends up with a slightly more modest 25 (28 with the meningitis C vaccine). In all the studies done of vaccination, epidemiologists have never investigated whether there is an upper limit to the number of jabs a baby can tolerate, after which all sorts of subtle damage—asthma, learning disabilities, hyperactivity or chronic earache, for instance—come into play. *In fact, nobody has done any long-term safety studies at all.*

Nevertheless, the American government, through its National Academy of Sciences, which surveyed all the scientific literature on each vaccine, has admitted that there is no such thing as a safe vaccine. The risks range from minor illnesses to permanent brain damage and death. It is not, we argue, that the vaccines don't work at all, but that they work imperfectly, and at an unacceptable cost to infant and child health. Vaccines might confer a temporary immunity and wear off at the point when exposure to the disease is most dangerous. Or they may have other health risks, including permanent disability and death, at rates far higher than those from contracting the disease naturally.

These pages provide copious evidence, now recognised by the medical profession in America, about the true risks and ineffectiveness of these vaccines, evidence that makes a lie of any health worker's blithe assurance that childhood vaccines are "perfectly safe". The chances are that your doctor won't tell you anything about this. The likelihood is that he may not even know, or he's been reading a variety of official books, whose unsupported and zealous conclusions are utterly at variance with a great deal of scientific fact.

At the heart of the logic behind vaccination is the theory of herd immunity—that is, if enough people get vaccinated against a certain disease, it will eventually disappear. Besides an element of wishful thinking in the face of highly complex organisms like viruses, which constantly mutate and change, the problem with this line of reasoning, of course, is its tyrannical approach: eliminating a disease is more important, in the eyes of medicine, than your child's health, which might be damaged from a vaccine, or your right to decide what is best for your family. Decide against vaccination for your child and you are considered not only an irresponsible parent but an irresponsible citizen of your community and even the world. In Britain, vaccinating your child is often a requirement for staying on your GP's list. (If he has 22 children under two on his list, say, he gets paid a bonus of about £2400 if 90 per cent of them are vaccinated. But if only 70 per cent are vaccinated, that bonus shrinks to about £800.) In the US, it is now more difficult than ever to get exemptions in your state for vaccination.

But in Britain, we still have a modicum of choice. In many countries all children are obliged to get vaccinated in order to get into school—a policy, particularly in places like America, that would seem to fly in the face of a number of constitutional freedoms. In this hysterical climate, the government and the medical community have made it their right to insist on administering a substance to a minor which it cannot guarantee is safe—a right no one has yet attempted to challenge in court.

It's likely that you've already heard the case in favour of immunisation. Hence, our writings make an unabashed case against it. This newly updated volume covers all the latest studies we've gathered on DPT, MMR, polio, Hib, BCG, hepatitis B, chickenpox, flu, the new meningitis C and travel vaccines. It also contains information about your legal rights, a consent form, prepared for us by our lawyer, which you can use to prevent your health authority from vaccinating against your will, and many solid alternatives to use if you decide against vaccination.

Our purpose is not to convince you not to vaccinate, but to help you exercise your right to choose, by giving you the other side of the story, so that your choice is really informed.

When dealing with individual vaccines we have narrowed our vision to three questions: "How necessary is it to vaccinate against the disease in question?" "How effective are these drugs?" and "How safe?" We've also concentrated on evidence published in the medical literature. If you are going to make a case against vaccination with your doctor, this is the kind of material he should respect.

With all our work on vaccination, we acknowledge our debt to the late Robert Mendelsohn and his editor Vera Chatz, who first enlightened us, like many other grateful disciples, about the risks of immunisation, back in the early 1970s. As the first American paediatrician to publicly denounce this most sacred of medical cows, Mendelsohn was the bravest man I have ever known.

We are also grateful to Dr J Anthony Morris, formerly a top American virologist at the Food and Drug Administration and National Institutes of Health, who developed many doubts about vaccination over the years and who regularly alerts us to many specific studies on vaccination. Dr Viera Scheibner of Australia provided some data on the MMR vaccine dangers, and Jane Colby and Doris Jones compiled material on the link between ME and the polio virus.

Finally, we are again grateful to our regular contributors: Clive Couldwell, Pat Thomas and Fiona Bawdon.

Lynne McTaggart

Chapter one

THE GREAT VACCINE MYTHS

Conventional medicine would have us believe that its faith in mass vaccination as a way of eradicating disease is based on hard scientific evidence. It isn't. The mythology surrounding vaccination doesn't stand up to close, objective analysis of the facts. Why is it then, you may ask, that every doctor you ever meet believes the myths about vaccination? Simply because every doctor he ever met believed them too and most won't have ever taken the trouble to examine the evidence for themselves. The other reason is that doctors themselves are educated about vaccination by drug companies and governments, both of whom have enormous vested interests in a programme that requires multiple drug purchases for virtually every infant in the country. A vaccine campaign makes a government look good by supposedly staving off epidemics and showing that it cares.

A blunt instrument

Vaccination is a blunt and highly imperfect instrument. The main problem isn't so much that vaccines don't work, but that they work haphazardly. The premise of vaccination rests on the assumption that injecting an individual with weakened live or killed virus will trick his body into developing antibodies to the disease, as it does when it contracts an illness naturally. But medicine doesn't really know whether vaccines work for any length of time. All that the usual scientific studies can demonstrate (as they are only conducted over the short term) is that vaccines create antibodies in the blood. What may happen is that a number of vaccines are capable of measurably raising antibodies to a particular infectious illness, but only for a short period of time. Or even if they do raise antibodies indefinitely, this may have nothing to do with protecting an individual from contracting the disease over the long (or even the short) term. For instance, large numbers of people who have had illnesses such as diphtheria never produce antibodies to the disease.

In one report, for instance, measles antibodies were found in the blood of only one of seven vaccinated children who'd gone on to develop measles—they hadn't developed antibodies from either the shot or disease itself (J Pediatrics, 1973: 82: 798-801). And lately, the Public Health Laboratory Service in London has discovered that a quarter of blood donors between 20 and 29 had insufficient immunity to diphtheria, even though most would have been vaccinated as babies. This percentage doubled among the 50-to-59 age group (Lancet, 1995; 345: 567-9).

The theory behind vaccination contains numerous flaws:
• It assumes that micro-organisms, rather than the overall health of the host, are primarily responsible for disease.
• It ignores the many instances where fully vaccinated individuals have nevertheless contracted the disease.
• It doesn't take into account large numbers of people who had illnesses such as diphtheria but whose bodies did not produce measurable antibodies.
• It doesn't ask what happens to live viruses over time. Numerous studies suggest that they consume large portions of the immune system, eventually causing auto-immune diseases such as multiple sclerosis.

- It doesn't take into account that vaccines may only work in a hit-and-miss fashion, conferring temporary immunity—the length of which no one understands.

There are four myths around vaccination which seem to be particularly pervasive:

- Diseases have been eliminated purely as a result of vaccination.

Wrong. Because the death rate from many infectious diseases declined, thanks to improved sanitation and hygiene, housing, better nutrition and isolation procedures, at around the same time vaccines appeared on the scene, the medical establishment has put two and two together and made five.

It has assumed that vaccination is entirely responsible for these diseases being cut down. It isn't. Take medicine's supposed greatest achievement. According to the medical textbooks, smallpox was eradicated through vaccination. However, examining the last century's epidemiological statistics you can see that between 1870 and 1872—18 years after compulsory vaccination had been introduced, and when 97.5 per cent of the population had been forcibly vaccinated—England experienced the worst smallpox epidemic of the century. Smallpox claimed 44,000 lives and three times as many people died from smallpox as had died in an earlier epidemic when fewer people had been vaccinated.

The town of Leicester refused to be vaccinated (after 1871), largely because the 1870 epidemic's high death rates convinced the town that vaccination didn't work. In the 1892 epidemic, Leicester relied solely on improved sanitation and quarantines. The town only suffered 19 cases and a death rate of one per 100,000 people. However, in Warrington, 99 per cent of whose population had been vaccinated, there were six times the number of cases. It also had 11 times the death rate of Leicester (Campaign Against Fraudulent Medical Research Newsletter, 1995; 2 (3): 5-13, quoting statistics from the London Bills of Mortality 1760-1834 and Reports of the Registrar General 1838-96, as compiled in Alfred Wallace, *The Wonderful Century*, 1898).

The World Health Organisation has highlighted the fact that eradication of smallpox in many parts of west and central Africa was down to switching from mass immunisation, which wasn't working very well, to a campaign of surveillance and containment (Bulletin of the World Health Organisation, 1975; 52: 209-22).

Sierra Leone's experience shows that vaccination didn't end smallpox's reign of terror there either. In the late 1960s, Sierra Leone had the highest smallpox rate in the world. It began an eradication campaign in 1968 and three of the four largest outbreaks were controlled by identification and isolation, not immunisation. Fifteen months later, the area recorded its last case of smallpox (BMJ, 1995; 310: 62).

More than any other, the polio vaccine is cited as proving that mass vaccination programmes work—but here again the vaccine may be taking credit that is not due. During the plague years of polio, 20,000-30,000 cases a year occurred in America, compared with 20-30 cases a year today. On the face of it, these figures seem impressive. However, Dr Bernard Greenberg, head of the Department of Biostatistics at the University of North Carolina School of Public Health, points out that cases of polio increased by 50 per cent between 1957 and 1958, and by 80 per cent from 1958 to 1959 after the polio vaccine was introduced (Walene James, *Immunization: The Reality Behind the Myth*, Massachusetts: Bergin & Garvey, 1988). In five New England States— Massachusetts, Connecticut, New Hampshire, Rhode Island, and Vermont—cases of polio roughly doubled in 1954 and

1955, after the vaccine was introduced (Neil Z Miller, *Vaccines: Are They Really Safe and Effective?*, Santa Fe, NM: New Atlantean Press, 1992).

The true explanation for the drop in the number of cases of polio is probably two-fold. It is partly due to the fact that diseases like polio operate cyclically. Like the 1950s outbreak, the two earlier great polio epidemics in the 1910s and 1930s were followed by a sharp dropping off of cases down to almost zero. But as the 1950s epidemic heralded the introduction of immunisation, it was this that took the credit, rather than nature.

Another factor in the reduction in the number of polio cases may simply be that the official figures are distorted as old diseases, like polio, are given new names, such as aseptic meningitis or coxsackievirus. According to statistics from the Los Angeles County Health Index, for example, in July 1955 there were 273 reported cases of polio and 50 cases of aseptic meningitis, compared with five cases of polio and 256 cases of aseptic meningitis a decade later (James, *Immunization*). Deaths from measles also declined by 95 per cent and whooping cough by 75 per cent before the vaccines were introduced (Miller, *Vaccines*).

• The diseases you are vaccinated against are deadly.

Wrong. The rationale for vaccination used to be to save lives by controlling a deadly disease. Increasingly, however, it is now being used to keep much milder, nuisance diseases at bay—childhood illnesses such as measles and even chickenpox. Although not so long ago these conditions were thought of as an inconvenient but fairly benign part of growing up, in the drive to encourage parents to vaccinate against them, they have turned into potential killers.

The supposedly killer diseases that vaccination is meant to protect against may be less of a threat than is often realised.

Even polio isn't the virulent mass killer its made out to be. Most cases are harmless infections (Richard Moskowitz, *Immunization: The Other Side in Vaccinations: The Rest of the Story*, Santa Fe, NM: Mothering, 1992). And whooping cough is no longer a serious threat to a well-nourished young child's health, according to Gordon Stewart, advisor to the WHO. The lesson of history—not just medical history—is that infectious diseases change in pattern, severity and frequency through time. Whooping cough was once a serious threat to life and health in all young children. Now it is no longer so, though it is often a distressing disease and dangerous in some infants, he writes (World Medicine, September 1984).

• Vaccines will protect you against these diseases.

Wrong. The vaccine lobby argues that the big benefits vaccines bring are worth the pain of the side effects. This argument assumes that vaccines work when, in reality, often they don't. For example, the whooping cough vaccine may work in only 36 per cent of cases. Dr Stewart reported that, in a study of whooping cough cases for 1974 and 1978 in the UK, and in 1974 in the US and Canada, a third to a half of all children who caught it had been fully vaccinated (Lancet, 1977; *i*: 234).

In the case of the BCG vaccine, the level of protection offered against TB can range from 80 per cent to none at all, according to 10 randomised control trials from around the world since the 1930s (Medical Monitor, June 5, 1992).

• The side effects of vaccines are rare and mostly mild.

Also wrong. We're only just finding out just how dangerous these vaccines are.

In the US, the government requested that the National Academy of Science review all the medical literature and report fully on what were the known and proven dangers, if any, of the then mandatory childhood vaccines. In two separate reports, the NAS's Institute of Medicine, which gathered together leading paediatricians and medical scientists for the task, concluded that all nine vaccines had the potential to do serious harm.

Several years later, the US Centers for Disease Control and Prevention, the highest American public body on infectious diseases, showed that a child's risk of seizure (epilepsy, convulsions and fainting) triples within days of receiving either the MMR or the DPT vaccines.

In the most definitive vaccines study to date, CDC monitored the progress of 500,000 children across the US and identified 34 major side effects to the jabs, ranging from asthma, blood disorders, infectious diseases and diabetes to neurological disorders, including meningitis, polio and hearing loss.

The CDC study was unable to determine whether these side effects were caused by something in an individual vaccine or whether giving so many of them all at once was causing, in effect, immune-system melt-down. It is planning further research to try to find out.

While we await the CDCs further findings, there is already plenty of evidence of the damage wrought by the individual components. For example, German authorities have discovered 27 neurological reactions to the mumps vaccine, including meningitis, febrile convulsions, encephalitis and epilepsy (Lancet, 1989; *ii*: 751). Canadian researchers estimated the risk of vaccine-induced mumps encephalitis at one per 100,000 (Can Dis Weekly Report, 1987; 13-35: 156-7); while a Yugoslavian study put it as high as one per 1,000 (Pediatric Infectious Disease Journal, 1989: 8: 302-8). The rubella shot can cause arthritis in up to 3 per cent of children and 20 per cent of adult women who receive it, according to one manufacturer (*The Physicians' Desk Reference*, 1995). On rare occasions, symptoms can last for years and range from mild aches to extreme crippling.

Vaccination has also led to the creation of new diseases, such as atypical measles, which can be more serious than the ones it is designed to protect against (see chapter 12).

Chapter two

WHAT VACCINES
ARE MADE OF

Avaccine is a complex mix of live or killed viral or bacterial antigens, or foreign invaders. Normally, when antigens enter your body, you produce antibodies, or blood proteins, which help the body recognise and destroy them. Remember: the premise that vaccination works rests on the assumption that introducing live or killed pathogens will trick the body into developing antibodies to the disease, as it does when it contracts an illness naturally.

Live vaccines are made from live pathogens that are attenuated (weakened) so that they won't cause symptoms of the full disease when administered. This is accomplished supposedly by sending these pathogens through a rather mystifying process called "serial passage", in which the viral strain is passed through up to 50 animal cells on the assumption that this will weaken them.

Not only the process but the cells selected appear a bizarre and arbitrary choice. Currently, the polio vaccine is passed through monkey kidney cells, the measles vaccine through chick embryo cells, rubella virus through rabbit or duck cells and yellow fever through mice and chick embryo cells (Jamie Murphy, *What Every Parent Should Know about Childhood Immunization*, Dennis, Massachusetts: Earth Healing Products, 1994). Human cells are also used; rubella has been grown on the tissue of aborted foetuses, and hepatitis B at one time was made from the blood of homosexual men who'd had the disease. Of course, this passage through animal and human cells invites infection or contamination with other substances, as happened with polio vaccines contaminated with SV40, a monkey virus, now thought to be responsible for a rare cancer (see Polio, chapter 4).

Among the childhood vaccines, the live vaccines include the tuberculosis (BCG), measles-mumps-rubella (MMR), the oral polio vaccine and the chickenpox vaccine. Among travel vaccines, the cholera, typhoid and yellow fever vaccines are also live. Many vaccines are made with live antigens because the killed versions haven't worked. The main concern with live vaccines is that the disease the vaccine is supposedly protecting against has a small chance of reproducing and spreading in the recipient.

Killed vaccines are made of components of the disease—whole cells, toxins, synthesised molecules, for instance—that have been rendered inactive with heat, radiation or chemicals. The Salk polio jab, the diphtheria-whooping cough (pertussis)-tetanus (DPT), hepatitis B and *Haemophilus influenzae B* (hib) meningitis are all among the most common killed vaccines.

The killed vaccine is supposed to preclude the possibility of the antigen being reproduced in the person receiving the vaccination—it is simply supposed to stimulate the circulation of antibodies to the antigen through the body. However, it's not quite as clearcut as this—serious problems with killed vaccines have defied their inability to reproduce in the recipient (Jamie Murphy, *What Every Parent Should Know about Childhood Immunization*).

Besides the antigens themselves, vaccines need to be cultured in a variety of substances to help them grow, to kill impurities, to help stabilise them and to boost their antibody-producing abilities. The three most common chemicals in vaccine production are thimerosal, a preservative derived from mercury; formalin (a 37 per cent solution of formaldehyde, the main ingredient of embalming fluid), included to inactivate viruses and detoxify toxins; and aluminium sulphate, an adjuvant, or vaccine-effectiveness booster, which is supposed to increase the ability of a vaccine to produce antibodies. Phenol (a disinfectant and dye), ethyene glycol, the main ingredient in antifreeze, benzethonium chloride, an antiseptic, and methylparaben, a preservative and antifungal, are also often added to the pot.

The only study that has tested the use of these substances has examined their effect on animals, and discovered that seven of the most commonly used substances have the ability to produce tumours (Clinical Toxicology, 1971; 4: 185, as reported in Murphy). In another study, examining the use of thimerosal similar to the way that it is used in vaccines, patients given immunoglobulin preserved with thimerosal had raised mercury levels in their bodies (BMJ, 1979; *ii*: 12). Ironically, Jonas Salk, who developed the killed polio vaccine, found that thimerosal actually inhibits the effect of the polio vaccine.

Each of these individual ingredients have been studied in other contexts and found to have many side-effects. Studies have shown that germicides like thimerosal have a negative effect on white blood cells (Am J Public Health, 1940; 30: 129, in Murphy), and of course aluminium is known to be toxic in drinking water. Mercury is among one of the most toxic substances in man (see *The **WDDTY** Dental Handbook*).

Studies have demonstrated that a large percentage of people have or develop allergic sensitivity to thimerosal, used as a disinfectant in vaccines. One study showed that more than a third of allergic patients undergoing allergy desensitisation with shots containing thimerosal developed hypersensitivity to the mercury salt (Contact Dermatitis, 1989; 20: 173-6). Some researchers have demonstrated that this high sensitivity to thimerosal is due to previous exposure to the substance in vaccinations (Contact Dermatitis, 1980; 6: 241-5). We also know that mercury salts can cause immune suppression in animals (Toxicology and Applied Pharmacology, 1983; 68: 218-28).

As for formalin, 47 studies have demonstrated an association between formaldehyde exposure and cancer, including leukaemia, and cancer of the brain, colon and lymphatic tissues (Randall Neustaedter, *The Vaccine Guide: Making an Informed Choice*, Berkeley, California: North Atlantic Books, 1996).

Since the 1940s, scientists have been experimenting with adjuvants to kickstart vaccines in working more effectively. Adjuvants work by trapping the vaccine in a pool and then drip-feeding it into the lymph nodes and spleen. Even the tetanus toxin is used as an adjuvant to boost other vaccines which don't work very well.

According to Kenneth Brown, commenting in an article published in the New York Academy of Sciences in 1995: "The body of knowledge regarding mechanisms of adjuvancy or adjuvant effect could better be described as voodoo or witchcraft."

Certain adjuvants appear to cause more reactions. In one study, there were higher side-effects with calcium phosphate rather than aluminium hydroxide and adjuvants in DT vaccines (Vaccine, 1995; 13: 1366-74). The adjuvants have varying effects on the protective ability of the vaccines; in one study, higher antibodies were developed with aluminium phosphate than sterol tyrosine or calcium phosphate (Biologicals, 1994; 22: 53-63). Oil adjuvants, used for example in the flu vaccine, have been shown to cause hypersensitivity, cysts and arthritis, and aluminium in vaccines may not only contribute to cysts and granulomas at the injection site, but to cancers and arthritis as well (Murphy, *What Every Parent . . .*).

Of the few studies that have been done on aluminium in vaccines, one shows that those containing aluminium cause more reactions. In one trial in Sweden, DPT vaccines containing aluminium causes the same number of reactions as shots containing the aluminium prepared as a adjuvant alone (Lancet, 1988, *i*: 955-60). Aluminium also appears to intensify allergic reactions to the whooping cough vaccine. In one study, children given the aluminium vaccine had more severe reactions such as fever, fretting, and redness and swelling at the injection site than those who'd had the plain vaccine. Furthermore, once given a booster shot, those given the aluminium vaccine showed their bodies were producing IgE antibodies to the whooping cough toxin, which indicates an allergic response (Pediatrics, 1989, 84: 62-7; Int Archives Allergy & Applied Immuno, 1989; 89: 156).

Scientists rarely address where the metals frequently used in vaccine production settle in the body. In a separate case study, two patients developed localised nodular reactions at the site of their anti-tetanus jab. Laboratory examination of the lesions showed the formation of granulomas, which when examined by special x-ray equipment showed the presence of aluminium and phosphorus in the granular debris (Am J Dermatopathology, 1993; 15: 114-7).

Besides these preservatives, many other substances get thrown in the pot. As Jamie Murphy describes in her excellent book, the DPT vaccine combines toxoids of diphtheria and tetanus with the whole cells of pertussis bacteria. Large amounts of diphtheria and pertussis are grown in a broth. Toxoids are the poisonous products of the tetanus and diphtheria organisms. These are produced in a stew of dextrose, beef heart infusion, sodium chloride and casein, cut with methanol, a raw alcohol, to purify it, then dissolved in a buffer. The final "ingredient" is the whole cells of the whooping cough, or pertussis bacteria. They are grown in large vats in a culture of minerals and casein, then killed by heat or thimerosal. After one or another adjuvants like aluminium are added, the stew is complete and ready for injection into a two-month-old baby.

But no one really knows the precise nature of the interaction of all these chemicals and toxoids; what we do know is that adding formalin to crude toxins polymerises impurities and bacterial antigens—that is, joins them together—(Randall Neufstader, *The Vaccine Guide*).

Perhaps the most telling description of vaccine production is Jamie Murphy's graphic account of the making of smallpox vaccine in the 1900s. A three-month-old calf would be pinned, while up to 50 inch-long incisions were made in the animal's stomach. Smallpox infection would be rubbed into the incisions and the animal returned to his stable and placed so that it would be unable to lick its sores. After a week, the animal would be infested with pus-laden smallpox pustules. Then the animal would then be returned to the operating theatre. "The smallpox crust," Murphy writes, "is then scraped from each sore with a blunt lancet, and the remaining contents of blood, skin, lymph and pus are drawn from each sore and transferred to a heat-resistant pot. Glycerine is added to the poisonous swill, and the entire contents are mixed with an electric motor. They are then passed through a sieve to removed the coarse materials (rotten flesh, hair etc.) and homogenised again. . . . The mixture is then poured into tubes and sold throughout the country as pure calf lymph, commonly known as smallpox vaccine."

Chapter three

DIPHTHERIA, WHOOPING COUGH AND TETANUS (DPT)

Whooping cough, caused by the *Bordetella pertussis* bacteria, causes a respiratory infection. The disease got its name from the whooping noise that victims make when they try to catch their breath. The illness lasts for three weeks and undergoes several stages. At first, breathing is difficult and then victims often have coughing attacks at night. Death, which is now rare, except among very young babies, is caused by inadequate oxygen during a coughing attack. It can take two or three months to recover.

No longer a dangerous disease

Dr Gordon Stewart, one of Britain's experts on whooping cough, believes that whooping cough is no longer a serious threat to life and health in children, other than some infants. During the whooping cough outbreaks of 1978-9 in Glamorgan, Glasgow and Surrey, in low-risk areas—that is, areas of adequate nutrition—there were no cases of permanent brain damage or death among any children, nor among any babies, who are considered most at risk (World Medicine, September 1984: 20).

Although it may no longer be dangerous, whooping cough is becoming an adult disease. More than 12 per cent of American adults are affected, whereas just 3 per cent were likely to catch the disease before mass vaccination programmes were introduced.

By vaccinating the very young, people over the age of 15 are more prone to develop whooping cough, which suggests the vaccine is merely suppressing the disease. It could also be that the vaccine itself is responsible for introducing the disease to an adult population. Rather than being prompted to rethink the validity of the shot, the researchers from the Kaiser Permanente Vaccine Study Center in Nashville, Tennessee, who carried out a study of the average age of whooping-cough incidence, responded by calling for more of it. They recommended that children over the age of seven should be given a booster shot (JAMA, June 5, 1996).

The dangers of DPT

Of all the adverse reactions from vaccinations now reported on the American Vaccine Adverse Event Reporting System, which was set up in the US to identify side-effects of vaccines, the overwhelming majority are due to the DPT vaccine.

During the period from January through August 1991, there were 3,447 reports of DPT reactions—66 per cent of over 5,000 reactions reported. Several recent events in the US have also made a mockery of medicine's continued insistence that the whooping cough vaccine (the P of the DPT or diphtheria, pertussis, and tetanus triple jab) is perfectly safe.

The Institute of Medicine at the National Academy of Science, a group of 11 leading paediatric figures in the US, spent 20 months reviewing hundreds of scientific papers. They concluded that the whooping cough vaccine can cause a number of health problems. The Institute's conclusions were conservative, and not supported by Dissatisfied Parents Together, an organisation of the parents of vaccine-damaged children which pushed through the US Vaccine Injury Compensation Program legislation several years ago.

Nevertheless, this is the first time that an American medical organisation has baldly stated on the record that the pertussis vaccine does damage some children.

The report was released right before a meeting of the Vaccine Advisory Committee, which produced a wealth of data about recurring problems with this vaccine, and the Vaccine Injury Compensation Program, set up to compensate victims of vaccine damage. Incredible as it seems, the safety of this drug was never adequately proved before being injected into millions of babies.

In the seminal work on the subject, *DPT: A Shot in the Dark*, (Avery Publishing Group, New York), medical historian Harris L Coulter and his co-author Barbara Loe Fisher describe the invention and development of the pertussis vaccine. Essentially, the vaccine as we know it today is no different from the first batches of it created in 1912. At that time, two French bacteriologists grew the pertussis bacteria in large pots, killed it with heat, preserved this stew with formaldehyde, and went ahead and injected it into hundreds of children. Today's vaccine still contains the whole cell of the pertussis bacteria, which is why its called a whole cell, or crude, vaccine.

One modern difference is the addition of an adjuvant, a metal salt (often an aluminium compound), to heighten the effect of the drug, plus a preservative, a mercury derivative. These ingredients are used despite the fact that formaldehyde is known to be a carcinogen, and aluminium and mercury are known to be highly toxic to humans (see chapter 2). The tetanus and diphtheria components were added both for convenience and after researchers noticed that the whooping cough component raised the efficacy of these vaccines.

The only safety test of the original whooping cough vaccine was conducted by the UK's Medical Research Council, which tried out the drug on 50,000 children of 14 months or older. The US never did do tests of its own, but has always relied on those conducted in the 1950s in Britain.

Furthermore, according to Coulter-Fisher, the 42 babies who had convulsions within 28 days of having been given the shot were discounted and the drug assumed to be safe, even though that level of reaction translates into about one in every 1,000 children. Though the trials were designed to demonstrate efficacy, not safety, US health authorities have used them as evidence that the vaccine was safe to give to babies as young as six weeks of age, says Coulter-Fisher. As has Britain. This means the drug was never tested for safety at this dosage for new-born children. It also means that two-month-old babies are given the same dosage as children three or four times their size.

Dr J Anthony Morris, long-time immunisation expert—formerly of the FDA—also pointed out in US Senate testimony that there is no consensus that the studies now performed on mice to prove individual lot safety are adequate. The statistics do not prove that the vaccine works particularly well in preventing the incidence of disease.

Pertussis vaccine doesn't work

The big argument put forward by apologists for the pertussis vaccine is that, imperfect as it may be, the benefits of preventing whooping cough are worth the risk. The problem with this argument is that it assumes that the vaccine actually works. According to health writer Leon Chaitow, author of *Vaccination and Immunization: Danger, Delusions, and Alternatives* (Essex: The CW Daniel Company, 1987), the great decline in deaths from whooping cough (some 80 per cent) occurred before the vaccine was introduced. The same holds true for diphtheria and tetanus, as a 1975 FDA-sponsored review of Bacterial Vaccines and Toxoids with Standards and Potency concluded, according to Robert Mendelsohn in *But Doctor. . . About that Shot.*

During outbreaks of whooping cough, half or more of the victims have already been fully vaccinated. Professor Gordon Stewart, formerly of the Department of Community Medicine at the University of Glasgow, reported that in a study of whooping cough cases in 1974-5 and 1978-9, and in 1974 in the US and Canada, one-third to one-half of all victims had been fully vaccinated. Furthermore, in studying 160 cases of infants contracting whooping cough, two-thirds of those who introduced them to the disease were their fully vaccinated siblings.

To his mind, no protection by vaccination is demonstrable in infants. This, despite the fact that the vaccine is primarily aimed to protect newborn children—usually the only ones whose lives are threatened by an otherwise relatively benign disease (Lancet, 1977; *i*: 234-7).

During a nationwide epidemic of whooping cough in 1993, a group of researchers in Cincinnati, Ohio, discovered that the vaccine is failing to protect children of all ages.

The researchers, from Cincinnati Children's Hospital, found that the epidemic mainly occurred among children who had completed the full course of DPT vaccines (New Eng J of Med, 1994; 331: 16-21). During that year, 6,335 cases of whooping cough had been reported, the most in 26 years. Of those, 352 cases were reported in Cincinnati, Ohio, a two-and-a-half times increase. About 30 per cent of the children had hospital stays, although the epidemic did not claim any lives. Of those affected, three-quarters had been given four or five doses of the DPT vaccine, and 82 per cent had received up to three doses, considered adequate to provide full protection.

As many of the children who contracted the disease were aged between 19 months and six years, even scientists have begun to agree that the whole-cell pertussis vaccine on offer does not offer long-term protection.

Similarly, in Finland, a recent study found that in a population with a 98 per cent immunisation rate, whooping cough infections remain common. Although the study found that whooping cough was common in pre-schoolchildren, the incidence was higher in schoolchildren and adults. This suggested that protection from the vaccine decreases over time (JAMA, 1998; 280: 635-7).

New research from Sweden (where whooping cough is a major problem, with epidemics peaking every year in the nation's children) and Italy has shown that the vaccine is effective in just 48 per cent and 36 per cent of cases, respectively (J Am Med Assoc, 1995; 274: 446-7).

Doctors are fond of pointing out that when the whooping cough vaccine was discontinued in the early 1970s in Britain for a time, the number of severe cases shot up. After a US documentary criticising the DPT vaccine, uptake levels of immunisation fell. Health officials then claimed that cases of whooping cough rose. But when Dr Morris, then of the US Institutes of Health, analysed 41 so-called cases, only five had true pertussis, and all of the victims had been vaccinated. The same occurred in Wisconsin for all but 16 of 43 cases and all of those had been vaccinated.

In Britain, cases rose to almost unprecedented heights, wrote Professor Stewart, in the 1978-9 epidemic. This was interpreted as having to do with the drop in vaccination following adverse publicity. But notification of cases increased in all age groups, including those where vaccination penetration had been high. Even those who believe in the whooping cough vaccine accept that its effect is unpredictable. In a statement to the Subcommittee on Investigations and General Oversight (IOM) in May 1982, Dr Morris said it has only been shown to be 63 per cent to 93 per cent effective—an extraordinarily large variable.

Diphtheria

The same seems to hold true with diphtheria and tetanus. Diphtheria is an acute respiratory infection caused by the *Corynebacterium diptheriae*. In its milder form, it may produce nothing more than a sore throat accompanied by fever and swollen lymph nodes. In severe manifestations, it can cause a thick membrane to form on the surface of the tonsils and throat, which may extend to the windpipe and lungs. Other complications include inflammation of the heart and paralysis of muscle in the throat and eyes. These complications can interfere with swallowing and breathing, leading to death in around 50 per cent of cases. In the pre-immunisation days people acquired immunity to the disease through contracting the less severe form. Infants were also likely to receive some degree of immunity, *in utero*, from their mothers.

According to Chaitow, quoting figures produced by the World Health Organisation, over 30,000 cases of diphtheria among fully immunised children have been recorded in the UK since World War II. An FDA-sponsored vaccine review concluded: "For several reasons, diphtheria toxoid, fluid or absorbed, is not as effective an immunising agent as might be anticipated." In the New Independent States of the Former Soviet Union during the early 1990s, the number of new cases reached epidemic proportions (JAMA, 1995; 273: 1250-2). By 1996, more than 100,000 cases of diphtheria had been reported (BMJ, 1996; 313: 502) and the vaccination programme did not appear to do any good. One research project showed that 86.3 per cent of those who were given the absorbed diphtheria-tetanus toxoid with reduced antigen content fell ill within a year after the first booster. The number of individuals unprotected on years three, four and five were 21 per cent, 35.5 per cent and 49.4 per cent respectively (Zhurnel Mikrobiologii, Epidemiologii i Immunobilogii, 1994; 3: 57-61). In October 1994, after this increase was noticed, it was recommended that all children age 15 to 18 years throughout Europe should receive a combined tetanus and low-dose diphtheria vaccine in place of tetanus vaccine alone. But in March 1995, 220 children aged between 14 and 16 were inadvertently given high-dose diphtheria with the tetanus vaccine. Most reactions were mild, but 31 per cent of the children reported at least one severe local or systemic reaction (BMJ, 1996; 313: 533-4).

Health-policy makers have reacted to news that vaccination hasn't wiped out the disease by promoting earlier and earlier immunisation of children in order to protect them. However, there is no research to show that early immunisation confers any benefit (Lancet, 1993; 342: 203-5), especially in relation to diphtheria. In fact, one study revealed that a DTP jab at birth actually lower the body's antibody response to diphtheria (J Ped, 1995; 126: 198-205). Neither does giving a pregnant women a DTP booster confer any benefit on her child. In one small study, the children of mothers given a booster during pregnancy had, initially, a lower immune response to diphtheria, even after their first two injections of DTP, although after the third booster their immune response jumped to normal (Ped Infect Dis J, 1995; 14: 846-50).

Tetanus
Tetanus is caused by *Colstridium tetani*, spore-forming bacteria, which get trapped in wounds that aren't cleaned properly. When the body is in the grip of tetanus infection,

the body muscles tighten, the jaw muscles go into spasms, making it difficult to open the mouth, and the patient suffers headaches, depression and convulsions.

The great fear about tetanus has always centred around puncture wounds (the proverbial rusty nail) or getting hurt on a farm in the presence of manure, which is supposedly riddled with tetanus spores. Although it is true that tetanus spores can grow in deep puncture wounds (because they do best in this type of an oxygen-free environment), cleaning the wound properly and not allowing it to close until healing has occurred below the skin surface will mostly eliminate the possibility of tetanus.

Long before the vaccine was introduced, deaths from tetanus were rapidly declining largely because of increased wound hygiene (Moskowitz, *Vaccinations:* 89). During the US Civil War in the mid-1800s tetanus occurred in 205 cases for every 100,000 wounds. However, 100 years later, during World War II, the incidence of tetanus declined by 99 per cent (Miller, *Vaccines:* 32). What that actually translates into is that among all the soldiers of the World War II, only 12 cases of tetanus were recorded—a third of which occurred among soldiers who were vaccinated (Science, 1978; 200: 905, in Miller). By the middle of this century, the disease was rare, but is now getting even rarer. By the 1970s, there were 20 notifications of tetanus a year in England and Wales; by the 1990s that figure had halved. In 1994, there were three notified cases and no deaths; the year before there had been three deaths of the six cases, all in women over 75. In the US, between 1985 through 1992 there were 467 cases of tetanus—an average of 55 cases a year (MMWR, 1993; 42: 768-70).

More than half of all untreated patients with tetanus supposedly die; however, we now know how to treat tetanus, and when treated correctly some 80 per cent of patients recover. This great decline in the incidence of tetanus has occurred despite the fact that immunity from the vaccine declines with age and a good percentage of the population aren't protected. In the latest community survey, conducted in Australia, of 430 randomly selected adults over 49, only half had levels of tetanus antibodies high enough to be considered protective. Furthermore, although 35 per cent of patients reported that they'd been vaccinated in the last 10 years, self-reported vaccination history didn't always correlate with a person's level of immunity (Med J Australia, 1996; 164: 593-6). Nevertheless, the incidence of tetanus is as rare there as it is in England (Lancet, 1996; 348: 1185-6), even though studies in England also find that elderly patients have lower levels of antibody protection (J Infection, 1993; 27: 255-60).

Once an infant has its tetanus shots, medicine recommends a booster every 10 years. However, there's evidence that the more shots you get, the lower your immunity. Each additional booster reduces the sensitivity of response to tetanus toxoid antigen after three or four challenges, according to a Lancet editorial (1996; 348: 1185-6). In another study, older people showed only 20 per cent protective immunity to tetanus (Age & Ageing, 1995; 24: 99-102). In fact, the elderly, who are most at risk from tetanus, have a far poorer take-up rate from the vaccine than do the young (J Gerontology, 1993; 48: M19-25).

Another factor lowering the effectiveness of vaccination is heavy levels of air pollution; antibodies to tetanus toxoid were found to be lower in children given three doses of the DPT vaccine who lived in German cities with high pollution, compared to control areas with less pollution (Zentralblatt fur Hygiene und Umweltmedizin, 1994; 195: 457-62).

Although studies of immediate response to tetanus

vaccination show very high protective antibody levels, this effect quickly wears off. In one study of 84 pregnant African patients, only 29 per cent had detectable antibodies in the blood, even though 74 per cent had been immunised within the three years preceding the study (African J Medicine & Medical Sciences, 1994; 23 19-22). Other studies show high detectable antibody levels of between 76-89 per cent after 10 years (Atencion Primaria, 1994; 14: 707-10). Although children may start out with high protective levels (97 per cent in children under five), this high protection wanes after adolescence.

Furthermore, as in many cases of vaccination, although antibody levels may be high, this may mean nothing in terms of protecting against disease. In one instance, an infant developed tetanus despite getting immunised and showing evidence of what were supposed to be protective levels of antitoxin antibodies (J Infectious Diseases, 1995; 171: 1076-7). In another study, five children between 5 and 15 contracted tetanus in Finland, even though four of the five had had their full quota of shots (Developmental Med & Child Neurology, 1993; 35: 351-5). Getting booster shots following injury may also be useless. One 66-year-old man sustained an injury to his right foot while gardening; despite receiving the shot and an adequate wound hygiene, he developed tetanus and died. The state of his immune system wasn't known (Medical J Malaysia, 1994; 49: 105-7).

A US-sponsored panel reviewing vaccines agrees that the vaccine has a spotty record of effectiveness. The panel noted that the degree of potency of the vaccine can vary considerably from preparation to preparation. The panel also concluded that, as the vaccine has been purified and made safer in order to prevent reactions to it, so its protective ability has diminished.

Even the weaker form of this vaccine has an impressive list of serious side-effects. The Institute of Medicines study of vaccine damage concluded that the tetanus vaccine could cause high fever, seizures, pain, nerve damage, fatal anaphylactic shock (a severe, life-threatening allergic reaction), degeneration of the nervous system and Guillain-Barre syndrome (Kathleen Stratton, et al. *Adverse Events Associated with Childhood Vaccines: Evidence Bearing on Causality*, Washington DC: National Academy Press, 1993: 261). The New England Journal of Medicine (1981; 305: 1307-13) reported that tetanus boosters can cause T-lymphocyte blood count ratios to temporarily plunge to below normal levels—similar to those of AIDS victims.

Another problem with this so-called safe vaccine is encephalitis or damage to the nervous system. *The Physicians' Desk Reference* warns that booster doses are more likely to increase the incidence and severity of reactions, if they are given too frequently. This is probably what happened to the 14-year-old son of Mary from Exmouth. He was given a tetanus injection following a dog bite. Five days later, he had his first epileptic fit at night, and he has had epilepsy ever since. Mary asked her GP if there was any connection between the two, but her fears were brushed aside and the boy's illness put down to coincidence. After all, her GP said, the tetanus vaccine is known to have no side-effects. "It was only when my son changed GPs a few years ago that his new doctor sent him for a brain scan to see if there were any underlying causes such as scar tissue," she said. "There were none."

In one instance, multiple sclerosis was triggered by a tetanus jab (Italian J Neurological Sciences, 1993; 14: 270). It's also been linked with encephalomyelitis (inflammation of the brain) (J Radiologie, 1996; 77: 363-6); plexus neuropathy (nerve abnormalities); a lowered immune system (Neurological Research, 1995; 17: 316-9); and Brown-Sequard syndrome, a form of paralysis (Tropical Doctor, 1994; 24: 74-5). A number of studies show that patients who already have high levels of antibodies have the worse reactions (Stratton, *Vaccines:* 70), and case reports link tetanus and diphtheria vaccine to arthritis and erythema multiforme (skin eruptions) (Stratton, *Vaccines:* 97).

Booster shots in older children also have demonstrated a high level of side-effects (Vaccine, 1994; 12: 427-30).

Even when the diphtheria and tetanus jabs are administered without the whooping cough component, side-effects are common. In one study of 139 Spanish medical students and health workers, 82 per cent of subjects recorded some kind of side effect, with 12 per cent reporting a systemic problem, such as malaise or headache (Med Clinica, 1995; 104: 126-9). More seriously, the DT jab on its own has been linked with encephalopathy in children—loss of consciousness, convulsions, headache and neurological problems (Bollettino dell Instituto Sieroterapico Milanese, 1984; 63: 118-124). In an English study of 18,000 children given three doses of DT, 18 children had febrile seizures, and three children suffered another neurologic disease, two with seizures. One of the three died of encephalopathy (Lancet, 1983; *i*: 1380-81).

DPT can cause brain damage

There is concern over the possibility of serious hypersensitivity reactions, such as skin rashes, swelling, itching and oedema, in association with diphtheria immunisation (J Immunol, 1997; 118: 334-41). Recent studies have shown that unusually high levels of IgE antibodies are stimulated by the DT vaccine (Vaccine, 1995;

13: 669-73) and that redness, swelling and itching were present in 73 per cent, 56 per cent and 47 per cent, respectively (Vaccine, 1994; 12: 427-30). Itching can persist for up to two weeks in some cases, and although some studies show that these symptoms are more pronounced with the DT vaccine, others show no difference in the severity of reaction between the DT and DTP vaccines (Acta Paed, 1994; 83: 159-63).

America now accepts that the DPT triple vaccine definitely can cause numerous health problems, and even kill. The IOM, which scoured the medical literature for 17 health problems that have been associated with the DPT vaccine, concluded that the evidence indicates a causal relation between administration of the vaccine and anaphylactic shock, extended periods of inconsolable crying or screaming, sometimes lasting 24 hours or more.

According to Coulter and Fisher, "this kind of crying, a thin, eerie, wailing sound quite different from the child's normal cry, [very much resembles] the so-called *cri encephalique* [encephalitic scream] found in some cases of encephalitis".

Of greater concern, however, is a link, albeit a weaker one, between the DPT vaccine and acute encephalopathy and shock, causing total collapse. This is not news. The link between the pertussis component in the DTP vaccine and encephalopathy was first raised in 1933.

Encephalitis is an inflammation of the brain, often referred to as meningitis, causing a bulging and red fontanel among infants. According to Coulter, many children either remain brain-damaged or die after these episodes. This is supported by the many interviews in his book, as well as the anecdotal evidence assembled by Dissatisfied Parents Together, where damage has occurred immediately following the vaccination.

Based on a review of 10-year follow-up data from the UK National Childhood Encephalopathy Study (NCES), the US IOM says the vaccine could trigger an acute neurological illness in children with underlying brain or metabolic abnormalities. An American doctor who tried to treat a boy of four says the boy suddenly started to display autistic characteristics within days of receiving the fourth in a series of childhood vaccines, which included DPT, Sabin polio and Hib. He had suffered fevers after the first three vaccinations, but nothing worse.

Until the fourth vaccine, his parents said he was very bright and affectionate, and had a vocabulary of 25 words. But after the fourth, he suffered vomiting, fever, lethargy and excessive sleepiness. After three days, he had an episode of inconsolable, high-pitched screaming (again, symptoms typical of the *cri encephalique*—see above). Immediately after this, he stopped talking, and there was a rapid change in his sociability. He also displayed repetitive behaviour and hand-flapping, all characteristics of autism. Medical tests revealed brain inflammation, although no neurologist would confirm the parents suspicion that the vaccine was the cause.

But, says Dr Harold Buttram, from Quakertown, Pennsylvania: "There are sound arguments that the vaccines administered at 18 months, especially the DPT vaccine, were responsible for the brain inflammation and autism."

The pertussis element of the DPT vaccine has long been suspected as a cause of many cases of autism, Dr Buttram says. The vaccine can depress or derange the immune system, especially in the very young.

Injuries to the immune system may at times be transferred directly to the brain, each having identical cell receptors, he wrote (Townsend Letter for Doctors, February/March 1996).

The federal government has concurred that on rare

occasions, permanent brain damage does occur. Doctors are now required to warn all responsible parties of vaccine recipients that pertussis vaccine may cause "lasting brain damage" (J Oklahoma St Med Assoc, 1996; 89: 135-8).

Researchers are also concerned that children can develop chronic brain dysfunction or even die if they develop an acute neurological illness within seven days of receiving the vaccination. The US IOM in 1991 estimated that there have been up to 10.5 cases of the condition per million vaccinations in excess of the expected rate. Although the committee said there was not enough evidence to conclude a relationship with various other disorders, it emphasised that they were not to be ruled out. These include: chronic neurologic damage, Guillain-Barre syndrome (a disease characterised by paralysis of the limbs), juvenile diabetes, learning disabilities, attention deficit disorder, infantile spasms and sudden infant death syndrome (SIDS).

There's also some concern that premature infants given the vaccine suffer from episodes of apnoea (that is, they stop breathing) (J Pediatrics, 1997; 130: 746-51).

In his US Senate testimony, Dr Morris mentioned an FDA support study at the University of California of children receiving a total of 15,752 doses of DTP vaccine. In the study, nine had convulsions, nine had episodes of collapse, a frequency for each of these conditions of one per 1,750 immunisations. Furthermore, there were two children who apparently fell victim to sudden infant death syndrome within 96 hours of the shot, which the authors concluded may have been related to the DPT vaccination.

As Dr Robert Mendelsohn pointed out in *But Doctor. . . About That Shot*, since each child receives three to five DTP shots, the true risk of damage is one per 400 children. In testimony before the US Senate Committee in 1985,

Secretary of Health Edward Brandt Jr estimated that every year 35,000 children suffer brain damage from this vaccine.

Another study in 1979 at UCLA estimated that 1,000 infants a year die from SIDS as a direct result of DPT, which represents some 10 to 15 per cent of the total number of SIDS deaths in America. This is borne out by the work of Dr Archie Kalokerinos and Glenn Dettman in studying aboriginal children. In the early 1970s, the researchers were puzzled when the death rate of aboriginal children skyrocketed, in some places to 50 per cent. Then they realised that the rise in the death rates coincided with intensified efforts to immunise these children, many of whom were ill or had serious vitamin deficiencies when they received the shots.

DPT and asthma

But this is only the merest inkling of the repercussions of our meddling. Dr Michael Odent and the Primal Health Research Centre in a study of long-term breastfeeding examined the number of children with asthma. If children were immunised against whooping cough they were six times more likely to have asthma as those who hadn't been given the jab.

This may have been what happened with the six-year-old daughter of Susan in Romney Marsh, Kent who took twice the recommended maximum dose of inhaled steroids for children and was recovering from whooping cough, despite being fully vaccinated as a baby.

"Her reaction to the first diphtheria-whooping cough-tetanus shot was to scream non-stop for 12 hours, a reaction we were told was normal. She was hospitalised with a high fever after the measles-mumps-rubella vaccine, after which she developed bowel problems, and then, after the DPT booster, full-blown asthma," said Susan. "We were talked into allowing her to be given two flu vaccinations. After that, she contracted one virus after another and numerous ear infections so that she was constantly on antibiotics. We feel that the inhaled steroids also had side-effects. She developed thinning shin, gained no weight at all in 18 months, and her feet stopped growing."

The acellular whooping cough vaccine

A new acellular version of the whooping cough vaccine (where the whooping cough toxin is inactivated by hydrogen peroxide, designed to make it safer), hasn't fared much better, either.

The US's new acellular, or partial cell, vaccine called DTaP has been approved by the US Food and Drug Administration since 1992, and now may be offered for babies, rather than simply as a booster shot for older children. The new variety is also being tested in Europe. Doctors are hoping that the results will assuage parents' fears about the safety of the shot.

In Sweden, where it was tested on a group of infants, one-fifth went on to develop whooping cough, even after they'd been given three shots. At best, the vaccine was judged to work less than three-quarters of the time (New Eng J Med, 1995; 333: 1045-50), and it was only 55 per cent effective after two doses. In America, scientists working on the vaccine at the Mayo Clinic have explained that they don't really understand how much pertussin toxin is necessary to protect children; even those with high levels of antibodies in their blood seem to go on and get whooping cough (Lancet, 1996; 347: 209-10).

Recent research suggests that the acellular vaccine may be no safer than the vaccine it's meant to replace. A large American study, named the Nationwide Multicenter Acellular Pertussis Trial, which compared over 2,000 children given either the acellular vaccine or the whole-cell version, found that the rate of serious adverse reactions—death, near-death, seizures, developmental delay and hospital stays—didn't differ between the old and new vaccines (Lancet, 1996; 347: 209-10).

A later Swedish study, which monitored nearly 100,000 children for two years, found that three versions of the acellular vaccine were far less effective than the whole-cell vaccine. Furthermore, the new vaccine appeared to carry as many side-effects as the whole cell vaccine. Convulsions were caused by both versions of the vaccine (Lancet, 1997; 350: 1564).

THE VACCINATION BIBLE

Chapter four

POLIO

The polio vaccine is often considered the essential shot, even among parents opposed to vaccination. More than any other, this vaccine is pointed to with pride by governments as proof that mass vaccination programmes work. Indeed, the polio vaccine has been called the safest vaccine known to man. But how safe is that?

The US government uses as evidence the fact that during the plague years of polio, 20,000 to 30,000 cases per year occurred in the US, compared to 20 to 30 cases a year today. But as Walene James points out in her book *Immunization: The Reality Behind the Myth*, Dr Bernard Greenberg, Head of the Department of Biostatistics of the University of North Carolina School of Public Health, has gone on record to say that polio *increased* by 50 per cent between 1957 and 1958, and 80 per cent from 1958 to 1959, after the introduction of mass immunisation.

Nevertheless, in the midst of the polio panic of the 1950s, statistics were manipulated by health authorities to give the opposite impression. One such way, says James, was to redefine the disease, renaming it "viral" or "aseptic meningitis", or "coxsackievirus". She quotes statistics from the Los Angeles County Health Index, for instance, showing that in July 1955 there were 273 cases of polio reported for 50 cases of aseptic meningitis, compared to five cases of polio in 1966 and 256 cases of aseptic meningitis.

In many cases, outbreaks of polio occur more among immunised than unimmunised populations. Taiwan suffered an outbreak of 1,031 cases of paralytic polio in 1982, even though some 80 per cent of infants there had received at least two doses of the oral vaccine before the age of one and at least 35 per cent of the victims had been vaccinated (Lancet, December 8, 1984). In the 1988 outbreak in Israel, of 15 cases, 12, or 80 per cent, had occurred among vaccinated individuals (Lancet, May 19, 1990: 1192-98). As most of the vaccinated victims were between 11 and 30, Israel's Defence Force Medical Corps concluded that this population suffered from a "gap" in immunity because they'd never been exposed to the wild virus (as people over 40 would have), but their vaccine had worn off (Vaccine, 1993; 11: 75-81).

According to Congressional hearings in 1961, Massachusetts had a polio outbreak with more paralytic cases among the vaccinated than the unvaccinated. "Every time we have an outbreak, the FDA blames it on a 'sub potent' vaccine," says immunisation expert Dr J Anthony Morris. "The fact is that many lots of the vaccine used fail."

Polio is not the virulent, mass killer it is made out to be. Largely because of the 1950s epidemic (following on four terms of the most highly publicised victim, President Franklin D Roosevelt) polio is popularly thought to cut down healthy young people randomly. In fact, most cases of polio are harmless infections. Polio is an enterovirus—that is, a gut bug—and there are types 1, 2 and 3. Most people experience fever, headache, aching limbs, sore throat and vomiting. It becomes a problem if the virus infects the nervous system, causing stiffness of the back or neck, joint pain and paralysis of either limbs or respiratory muscles. Fatalities occurred from the latter, when victims couldn't breathe. However, the current statistics estimate that only 10 per cent of people exposed to polio will contract it, and only 1 per cent of those will come down with the paralytic variety—or 0.01 per cent of those exposed to the disease in the first place.

Medical homoeopath and noted vaccine critic Dr Richard Moskowitz has called this tendency to develop paralysis from this ordinarily harmless virus a "special anatomical susceptibility". The reason behind a renewed fuss over the vaccine has to do partly with the difference in the way the two varieties of the vaccine work.

Killed IPV versus live OPV

Jonas Salk developed a killed viral vaccine, and Albert Sabin founded the live virus—used mostly in England and America. Both live and killed viruses work on the same principle—that is, they contain altered, supposedly safe forms of the three major strains of the wild polio virus.

When administered to a patient either by injection (the inactivated polio vaccine, or IPV) or orally (the oral polio vaccine, or OPV) they trick the body into creating antibodies, which allegedly "recognise" and counteract the real thing if they ever come in contact with it.

In true cases of polio, the virus lives in the intestine, creating what is ordinarily a harmless infection. The problem arises if it travels via the bloodstream to the nervous system, which is when it causes paralysis.

Jonas Salk's killed virus, injected under the skin, is supposed to travel to the bloodstream and create antibodies there, which will "block" the virus before it reaches the nervous system. However, the IPV does not give you "gut immunity"—that is, does not raise antibodies in your intestines. That means that while you won't get paralytic polio, the wild virus could live on in your gut and you could theoretically pass it on to someone else.

Furthermore, the original Salk vaccine required three or more boosters every five years.

At first, the Salk vaccine was deemed a terrific success—until the polio victim rate went up in the 1960s. Coming so shortly on the heels of the double-digit victim rates of the 1950s, this development was greeted as proof that the Salk vaccine didn't work, particularly amid all the hysteria to find a "cure", and the live virus was introduced.

The live oral vaccine became the vaccine of choice largely so that you or your children would act as an immunising force for other, unvaccinated individuals. Sabin's live vaccine came into use in the 1960s, virtually replacing the Salk vaccine, because it not only supposedly confers life-long immunity on its recipient, but also stops him from becoming a carrier of the wild virus. And because recipients can excrete the vaccine virus for a number of weeks through the mouth and faeces, the theory is that you can pass on immunity to non-vaccinated individuals, thus raising the "herd immunity".

The problem is that in some cases, this "attenuated" or weakened version of the vaccine virus genetically alters in the gut, transforming into its virulent form and causing paralytic polio in its recipient or those with whom the recipient has recently come into contact. These days, virtually the only cases of polio that occur in Britain or America from the vaccine are among those who come into contact with an individual who has been vaccinated, say, grandparents, parents, or siblings whose immunity from the vaccine has worn off or who are in some way susceptible.

According to ASM News (1988; 54: 560-2) there have been more than 100 cases of vaccine-induced paralytic polio in America between 1975-84. In the UK, 13 cases have been substantiated between 1985 and 1991 (British Med J, 1992; 305: 79-81). The US Centers for Disease Control in Atlanta estimates the current risk for vaccine-induced polio is at five per million doses given or one case for each 200,000 first doses, which are said to be the most risky (Lancet, 1984; *ii*: 1390). Among immuno-compromised people, that risk multiplies 10,000 times. In Germany, most of the cases of vaccine-induced paralytic polio have been among children aged two years or younger—that is, the recipients themselves.

This paralytic disease is known as vaccine-associated paralytic poliomyelitis—VAPP (Amer J of Pub Health, May 1996; 86: 734-7). The current risk is estimated to be between one case per 1.4m-2.5m in the US and UK (Bull WHO, 1995; 73: 33-40). In Germany, the risk is estimated at one per 200,000 doses (Lancet, 15 December, 1984). Among immuno-compromised people, that risk multiplies 10,000 times.

It's also five to 17 times higher in countries using large numbers of injections, causing "provocation" polio (New Eng J of Med, 1995; 332: 500-6).

Side-effects of the polio vaccine

Besides polio, your child also risks poor weight gain or other paralytic diseases with the vaccine. According to a report in the American Journal of Clinical Nutrition (1977; 30: 592-8), children immunised with live agents, such as the polio vaccines "suffered statistically significant reductions in their weight-for-age, compared to matched, non-immunised controls". Those who were smaller anyway were especially affected. The report ended up recommending that live vaccines only be given in developing countries in actual epidemics or if vaccination was otherwise difficult to achieve.

Recently, a new disease has been appearing in China, which the medical press has dubbed "Chinese paralytic syndrome" (CPS). Although it was previously diagnosed as the paralytic condition Guillain-Barre syndrome (GBS), researchers from the Second Hospital of Hebei Medical College in the People's Republic of China studied all the cases in depth and concluded that the disease, which strikes children and young adults, was a variation of polio.

Before the oral polio vaccine was introduced in the Hebei province in 1971, illness from polio was high, but diagnoses of GBS were uncommon. Then after 1971, the incidence of polio gradually fell, but that of GBS increased about tenfold. Three rises in the incidence of polio utterly coincided with three epidemics of GBS.

According to Yan Shen and Guohua Xi from the hospital's department of neuropsychiatry, the evidence strongly suggests that the polio virus is responsible for the cases diagnosed as GBS. "The widespread use of OPV may have led to [mutation of the virus], resulting in an alteration of [the disease] and/or to a change in the main epidemic type of polio virus," they wrote (Lancet, 1994; 344: 1026). In Brazil, 38 cases of paralysis classified as Guillain-Barre syndrome were analysed and, in all cases, the polio vaccine strain was isolated (Revista Do Instituto De Med Trop De Sao Paolo, 1996; 38: 55-8).

In Brazil, 38 cases of paralysis classified as Guillain-Barre syndrome were analysed and in all cases, the polio vaccine strain was isolated (Revista Do Instituto De Med Trop De Sao Paulo, 1996; 38: 55-8).

Cases of GBS linked to the polio vaccine also occur in the UK. Emma Whitlock went to her doctor's surgery in July 1991 to get a routine polio and typhoid vaccination for her family's upcoming trip to Morocco. She says: "That evening I developed a temperature, with aches and pains in my arms and legs. The pains in my legs were the most severe. About two weeks later, while I was out walking, one of my legs 'gave out'. It felt as though my legs were both weak, and they were numb. Sometime after that, my legs started to feel as though they were burning.

"My condition steadily deteriorated over the years, and I am now at the stage of being able to take only a few steps before I experience the pains and a horrible numbness in my legs, which forces me to sit down. Any kind of movement gives me the same pain, even if I travel in a car.

"My hands were affected, too. They now burn when I have done too much, and there is a weakness there. Besides the limb problems, I suffer earaches and a kind of deafness, plus frequent infected neck glands, which only clear up with antibiotics. I also have serious problems with balance, unsteady walking and falling. I have memory loss and often stop in mid-sentence.

"These effects have all had a devastating effect on my life. I am now totally house-bound. I have been resting solidly for nearly five months to try to get the burning pain to ease. Although it has eased somewhat, the pain and numbness are constant when I attempt to walk.

"Doctors have now diagnosed the problem as Guillain-Barre syndrome. When I contacted someone from the Guillain-Barre Society, he told me that I was the worse case he's ever seen. My doctor now admits that this was brought on by the vaccine."

Finland, like Sweden and The Netherlands, has always favoured the killed vaccine. However, following an outbreak of 10 cases in 1985, the government organised a mass vaccination campaign with the live vaccine. A few weeks after the campaign, the Department of Paediatrics at the University of Oulu in Finland, writing in The Lancet (August 19, 1989), reported a cluster of 27 cases of childhood Guillain-Barre syndrome, which also occurred in America following mass immunisation with the swine flu vaccine in the 1970s. Eleven of the Finnish children had been immunised before the onset of symptoms.

How effective is the vaccine?

Because the vaccine arrived as a white knight amid the polio epidemics of the 1950s, much of the success of polio vaccine and its high efficacy is taken for granted. Consequently, studies among Western adults—and any objectivity on the subject—are particularly hard to come by.

The effectiveness of the polio vaccine is supposedly demonstrated *de facto*—by the virtual disappearance of the disease in countries in the West that have introduced mass vaccination. However, a number of facts question this basic assumption. In all the major outbreaks of polio that have occurred in areas after mass vaccination began, a substantial number of cases, if not the majority, occur among the vaccinated.

Scientists now realise there is little evidence that the live vaccine actually does achieve the so-called "backdoor" immunity among the unvaccinated. This was the conclusion of a scientific study group after an outbreak of 1,000 cases of polio in Taiwan, despite the fact that some 80-98 per cent of young children had been immunised. The few studies carried out these days on the polio vaccine in infants in developing countries show a less than perfect take-up rate. The vaccine failed to give adequate protection to babies in the Gaza (Is J of Med Science, 1995; 31: 49-53); and less than two-thirds of Mayan, Gambian and Brazilian infants have produced antibodies to the type 3 virus after being vaccinated, according to separate studies (J Infect Dis, 1997; 175: 545-53 and 1995; 171: 1097-106). Some of the factors linked with vaccine failure included vaccination during the rainy season, diarrhoea at the time of vaccination, high levels of maternal antibodies and even breastfeeding. In other words, a mother's own antibodies might act to neutralise the potency of the vaccine. This leads one to speculate about how effective the polio vaccine is among infants in developed countries who are breastfed long-term.

Furthermore, even if the vaccine "takes", you may not be adequately protected against a certain strain of the virus. During a major outbreak of hepatitis A infection in Glasgow, the blood of 24 of the victims was also tested for antibodies to polio. Only one-third of the group had an acceptable level of antibodies against the type 3 strain (Br Med J, 1992; 304: 52).

There is also some evidence that the vaccine wears off quickly. In a study of 86 children who'd had either the enhanced killed or live vaccine, and were monitored for four years, each group showed a 10- to 100-fold decline in antibody levels to all virus types within the first two years of follow up (J Infectious Diseases, 1993; 168: 452-4). Those receiving two or more doses of the killed vaccine showed better immunity than those receiving the oral vaccine. In Thailand, there are still significant failure rates with the oral polio vaccine and a waning of immunity within six months after a full course of the vaccine (Scand J Infect Diseases, 1994; 26: 731-8).

HV Wyatt of the Department of Community Medicine at the University of Leeds has made the astonishing connection between multiple injections of any variety given to small children and the onset of polio, particularly in developing countries where children receive more shots than those in developed countries (Transactions of the Royal Society of Tropical Medicine and Hygiene, 1985; 79; 355-8 and 1989; 83: 545-9). Wyatt has made a career of studying different populations through this century, comparing injected drug treatment and epidemics of polio. These included studies of children in the early part of this century receiving injections for congenital syphilis.

He concluded that multiple injections may be responsible for 25 per cent of paralysis during epidemics of polio and making children 25 per cent more susceptible to the disease during non-epidemic periods.

A single injection, he found, could increase the risk of paralysis five-fold, and turn what would have been a non-paralytic attack into a paralytic one. Wyatt also believes that the risk might be cumulative—that is, multiple injections over time or a close interval between jabs might increase the risk of contracting polio at some point in the future.

Wyatt's thesis provides much food for thought about the origins of the great polio epidemics of this century, which may have been helped by the introduction of widespread vaccination and penicillin. His thesis has been validated by a study in Romania (where outbreaks have been occurring for the past 20 years), showing that the polio vaccine, given by injection, is causing outbreaks of the disease. While the shot itself appeared to have triggered paralysis, the children affected had been exposed to a large number of other injections of vaccines and antibiotics. The researchers, from the US Centers for Disease Control and Prevention, believe that the children risked paralysis if such injections had been given less than 30 days before the polio jab (New Eng J of Med, 1995; 332: 505-7). German doctors from the University of Cologne tacitly acknowledge the threat of provocation polio by recommending that it be given on its own, separate from other vaccines: "Since simultaneous intramuscular injections may increase the incidence of paralytic poliomyelitis, injections such as diphtheria-tetanus immunisation should not be given at the same time as OPV" (Lancet, 15 December 1984).

Victims of the live vaccine

These days, the cases of polio that occur in Britain or America, besides those from travellers, occur in the vaccinated—or those who come into contact with them.

Bernard Reis, an English professor at Vassar College and former graduate of Cornell University and Harvard, described as an "energetic, athletic achiever", was happily married with a baby boy who dutifully received the mandated vaccines.

A month after his little boy's vaccine, Bernard became tired attempting to climb a flight of stairs and came down with what he thought was flu. Two days later, he collapsed on his bathroom floor, and after being rushed to the hospital was completely paralysed, placed on an iron lung and fed intravenously. Eleven months later, he returned home in a wheelchair.

"The strain of all this was too much for my marriage, which fell apart," he wrote in The Washington Star.

Since then, he said, his life has been "hell in slow motion". Although able to walk haltingly, he is still extremely weak. He lives on Social Security of $300 per month in New York public housing. He has not been able to receive compensation from the drug manufacturer.

On 19 February 1984, the first day Bill and Debbie Miller were to move into their new home, Bill collapsed on the sofa. The following morning, he complained that he couldn't move his left arm. A few days later he was completely paralysed.

Months and a battery of tests later, they finally diagnosed Bill as having paralytic polio. His daughter had received her live polio vaccine less than two months before. No doctor had warned Bill, who was taking cortisone for the skin condition Netherton's Syndrome, that he was immuno-compromised and at high risk of contracting polio from a vaccinated person. This was despite the warning to physicians in packages from Lederle, the drug manufacturer.

Six months went by and his condition did not substantially improve. By October, he went into a coma and began bleeding internally. Four days later, his wife buried him.

On a bus ride to Minnesota for Christmas, 31-year-old Kay McNeary, travelling with her two small children, began to feel pains in her legs. Once she got to her parents, she took a hot bath and lay down. That was the last time she ever got up; a few days later she was crippled by polio.

In 1982, a Seattle jury determined that she caught the disease when she changed her daughter's nappy, right after the baby had received her OPV, and awarded her $1.1m.

This paralytic disease is known as vaccine-associated paralytic poliomyelitis—VAPP (Amer J of Pub Health, May 1996; 86: 734-7). The current risk is estimated to be between one case per 1.4m-2.5m in the US and UK (Bull WHO, 1995; 73: 33-40). Among immuno-compromised people, that risk multiplies 10,000 times.

It's also five to 17 times higher in countries using large numbers of injections, causing provocation polio (New Eng J of Med, 1995; 332: 500-6).

Live vaccine precautions

If you decide to immunise your baby with live polio vaccine after all, make sure you do the following:

• Have your and your family's immunity to polio checked out.

• For the three months following your child's vaccine, ensure you wash your hands carefully after all nappy changes.

• Make sure that your child avoids contact with any of the following groups at high risk of contracting vaccine-induced polio: those receiving radiotherapy, cytostatic drugs, systematic glucocorticoids, like cortisone, potent corticosteroids to the skin, and those taking ACTH or other immunosuppressive drugs; those with congenital immuno-deficiencies; those with a history of paralytic disease.

If you or any other adults wish to be vaccinated, consider having the killed jab, as the live one is considered riskier for adults.

Travel and the polio vaccine

The polio vaccine is the one vaccine urged on all travellers outside the West. However, the UK Department of Health's line on when you need a booster dose is broad-brush, to say the least. The DoH recommends that everyone travelling outside North and Western Europe, North America, Australia and New Zealand should be immunised. Anyone who hasn't been immunised against polio should get a full course of three doses, and anyone who had their vaccine more than 10 years ago should get a booster vaccine. This policy places luxury hotels on islands in the Caribbean on a par, in terms of risk of polio, with countries like Egypt in the summer months.

But how real a threat is polio? In the last decade, there have been no more than two cases a year in the UK. This is a remarkably low number considering the number of travellers in the UK who would have trooped to high risk areas without thinking to get a polio booster.

Other areas besides western Europe and North America are now virtually polio free, including the Arabian peninsula, the Pacific basin and southern Africa (Biol, 1993; 21 (4): 327-33). Nevertheless, there are still thousands of polio cases each year in many developing countries in Africa, Asia, the Middle East and Eastern Europe. It is also true that the average person under 40 living in the West may not have been exposed to wild polio virus and so has not built up natural immunity.

There is also evidence that the polio vaccine doesn't protect as well as it should in travellers. Three of the five Americans in one study who caught polio during foreign travel had been previously vaccinated against the disease (Clin Infectious Diseases, CDC, February 1992: 568-79).

If you are reluctant to get the vaccine, and you are travelling to an area at risk, it may be prudent to establish the true incidence of polio in the countries you are visiting and then avoid travelling in the warmer months, when the disease has its highest incidence.

If you have had a vaccine before and wish to avoid exposing yourself to the risks of another one needlessly, you can request a blood test to measure antibody response before getting a booster you don't need.

Chapter five

MEASLES, MUMPS & RUBELLA (MMR)

Until recently, some 93 per cent of pre-school children in Britain were pressed into receiving the live triple vaccine for measles, mumps, and rubella—German measles—the so-called MMR.

In 1994, the Department of Health laid aside £20m to invest in a programme to vaccinate children aged from five to 16 years against measles and rubella (MR). Even those who have had true measles (which offers lifelong immunity), or have already been immunised, were given a just-in-case booster shot. The British government resorted to television and newspaper scare advertising which suggested that measles is a deadly, debilitating disease.

In America, it has been suggested that welfare payments could be withheld from any mother refusing to vaccinate her child. Childhood shots have been given a further boost by the administration's Childhood Vaccine Act, which now makes it more difficult to get exemptions from vaccination in the US.

Just how dangerous is measles?

Measles, caused by a viral member of the paramyxovirus group, affects the respiratory system and the skin, causing itchy, pink spots over the body, runny nose, sore eyes that are sensitive to light and high fever. The zeal for vaccination is presumably founded on the belief that measles can be a life-threatening condition and, according to the statistics being banded about, it seems to be one that is getting more dangerous by the year.

When the Department of Health ran its last major vaccine drive in 1989, Dr Norman Begg, consultant epidemiologist of the Public Health Laboratory Service, cited the then official statistics that one in 5,000 children contracting wild measles will develop acute encephalitis, an inflammation of the brain; and one in 5,000 of those will develop SSPE (sub-acute sclerosing panencephalitis), an almost inevitably fatal progressive disease which causes hardening of the brain.

Five years later, when one columnist encouraged parents to have their children re-vaccinated in the countrywide measles campaign, the percentage of measles victims who might go on to develop encephalitis had shrunk to one in every 500. One in 10 of these will die and one in four will suffer permanent brain damage, the columnist maintained. As the campaign intensified, other newspapers had magnified the danger even further. By November, it seemed that one out of every 17 cases of measles would turn into a case of encephalitis.

But the report of the journal geared specifically for the study of the fatal illness being worried over, the SSPE Registry, concluded that the measles-induced form of this disease is "very rare", occurring in one per million cases (JAMA, 1972; 220: 959-62). Furthermore, a study of 52 people with SSPE concluded that environmental factors other than measles, such as head injuries or close exposure to certain animals, played an important part in the onset of the disease (Amer J of Epid, 1980; *iii*: 415-24): "There were no differences with regard to the average age at vaccination, having received more than one measles vaccination, or having received measles vaccine after natural measles," concluded the authors.

Measles is not the random killer that medicine would have us believe. In America in 1990, at the height of a measles epidemic when 27,000 cases of measles were reported, 89 people died. But what the government didn't tell you was that most deaths occurred among children of low-income families where poor nutrition played a part, as did failure to treat complications.

Deaths from measles are common in some European countries and this is directly related to poor vaccine coverage. according to Norman Begg (BMJ, 14 February 1998).

Deaths from measles are *not* common in developed countries. The year before the MMR vaccine was launched, there were six deaths from measles in Britain, even though there were 42,165 cases reported of the disease. Furthermore, in the five years between 1989 and 1994 there were only six deaths among children aged 0-19, even though there were a total of 59,263 cases of measles in this time period—an average of one death a year. This represents an incidence of approximately one death for every 10,000 cases, which is almost half that of the incidence from 1979-1983, when 83 children died out of 467,732 cases of measles, or about one death for every 5,600 cases. This lowered death percentage does not have any bearing on the vaccine, but reflects the fact, according to Dr Richard Nicolson, editor of the Bulletin of Medical Ethics, that doctors better understand how to treat measles. Since 1988, most deaths have occurred among adults, although again there are only a handful every year.

Deaths from measles are *not* common in developed countries. The year before the MMR vaccine was launched, there were six deaths from measles in Britain, even though there were 42,165 cases of measles in this time period—an average of one death a year. This represents an incidence of approximately one death for every 10,000 cases, which is almost half that of the incidence from 1979-83, when 83 children died out of 467,732 cases of measles, or about one death for every 5,600 cases. This lowered death percentage does not have any bearing on the vaccine, but reflects the fact, according to Dr Richard Nicolson, editor of the Bulletin of Medical Ethics, that doctors better understand how to treat measles. Since 1988, most deaths have occurred among adults, although again there are only a handful every year.

Norman Begg has recently written that deaths from measles are "directly related to poor vaccine coverage." Recently, The Lancet published a review article, written by a joint team from the US Centers for Disease Control and Prevention (CDC) and the Public Health Laboratory Service (PHLS) Communicable Disease Surveillance Centre, attempting to demonstrate that in areas where high coverage with the DPT vaccines was maintained (such as Hungary, Poland and the US), the incidence of whooping cough was 10 to 100 times lower than in countries where immunisation was "disrupted" and programmes "compromised" by "anti-vaccine movements" (their words). This idea—that it is only the anti-vaccine "element" that disrupts the efficacy of whooping cough vaccines—betrays a shocking distortion of the truth. For one thing, earlier in January, Dutch scientists were puzzling over the fact that Holland had suffered an epidemic of whooping cough, despite vaccination rates as high as 96 per cent—comparable to America's. Furthermore, there was no clustering of cases among the unvaccinated. The same is happening in Norway and Denmark.

Furthermore, in Italy, there were just 10 deaths from measles between 1989-91, even though they had only a 40 per cent coverage from the vaccine. In the following two years in Italy, coverage from the vaccine grew, but deaths nearly tripled to 28, suggesting that vaccine coverage had absolutely no bearing on numbers of deaths (BMJ, 1998; 316: 561). Well-nourished children have little to fear from catching measles—and possibly much to gain.

According to the very latest research, measles may be good for children. Researchers have discovered that African children who catch measles tend to suffer less from allergic conditions, such as asthma, eczema and hay fever. This is in contrast to children in developed countries who, while supposedly protected from the usual childhood diseases by vaccination, go on to suffer a range of allergy-related (atopic) conditions in increasing numbers.

Earlier research indicated that childhood diseases, such as measles, mumps and rubella, might provide natural desensitisation against atopy—hypersensitivity to common allergens. More recently, researchers from Southampton General Hospital in England discovered that measles may prevent atopy after studying 262 young people, aged between 14 and 20, from Guinea-Bissau. All of them had had measles, and the researchers tested their levels of sensitivity with skin-prick tests.

Just 12 per cent were atopic, compared to 26 per cent in another group who had been vaccinated against measles and so had not caught the disease. Researchers also noted that children who had been breast-fed for more than a year were less likely to have a positive skin test to housedust mite, thought to be one cause of asthma.

Interestingly, the scientists were only proving what the mothers already knew. The mothers seemed to know exactly who had contracted measles during an epidemic in the country in 1979 just by seeing who suffers from allergies today. Tests showed that they were invariably right (Lancet, 29 June 1996).

Does MMR really immunise against measles?

One catalyst for the 1994 MR advertising blitz in Britain, paradoxically, was the fact that no form of the measles portion of the vaccine was working as a one-off shot. Not long ago, America suffered its worst measles epidemic for decades, despite the fact that the measles vaccine in its various forms has been used since 1957 and the combined shot since 1975.

With immunisation rates as high as 98 per cent in some areas due to enforced vaccination, epidemics of measles still occur at three- to four-year intervals. Although the government targeted 1982 as the date of the virtual elimination of the disease, the CDC in Atlanta reported a provisional total of 27,672 cases of measles in 1990, which represents a virtual doubling of cases from 1989, which were double the number of cases from the year before that.

Although the number of measles cases fell by one-quarter to 63,000 the year the vaccine was introduced and bottomed out at 1,500 reported cases in 1983, the numbers suddenly swelled by 423 per cent at the end of the last decade, with the worst hit areas of the US being Houston, Texas and Los Angeles County. In Israel, nearly 1,000 cases were reported in 1994, despite an immunisation programme that, while voluntary, nevertheless covered about 90 per cent of young children in the target group.

The medical establishment has attempted to place the blame for the recent epidemic on clusters of the unvaccinated, particularly among poor, non-white populations, but the statistics prove otherwise. Of the 1989 CDC statistics, half the college-aged victims had been previously vaccinated. And between 1985 and 1986, two-thirds of all measles cases occurred in school-aged children, the majority of whom had been vaccinated.

Some theorise that the vaccine wears off in time, as does an individual's immunity, or that those vaccinated between 1957 and 1980 received a less stable version of the vaccine. Other theories blame the problem on shots given too early, which were interfered with by residual maternal antibodies acquired in the womb; or shots given when children have respiratory infections; or put the blame on vaccines badly stored or handled. This failure rate is largely responsible for the recent recommendation of a pre-school booster at age four or five.

Some medics believe that even two doses won't be enough to deal with the various "wild" strains around. Booster shots often don't work, either. In one study, previously vaccinated individuals lacking any evidence of immunity were given measles booster shots. Only half of them ended up with antibody levels considered protective (Pediatric Infectious Disease Journal, 1994, 13:34-8).

Not surprisingly, all the pro-vaccine researchers and government officials pass lightly over the fact that measles epidemics continued to occur consistently in fully vaccinated children. They also ignore the fact that measles is suddenly becoming an adult disease.

By 1975, once mass measles vaccination was offered, not only was the number of reported cases of measles six times higher in the first half of 1975 compared with 1974, but more and more adults were contracting measles (JAMA, 1976; 235: 1028-31). Not even booster vaccination of previously vaccinated children made any difference. One study in 1979 warned of an increasing number of adolescents contracting measles. While in the pre-vaccine era 90 per cent of all measles patients were five to nine years old, once the measles vaccine was introduced, 55-64 per cent of measles patients were older than 10 years. The average age of patients during a measles outbreak in a California university was 20-24 years (Ann Int Med, 1979; 90: 978-80). Furthermore, once vaccines were introduced, whether or not a patient had measles or had been vaccinated didn't seem to correlate with what was generally considered evidence of immunity in the blood. Revaccination of these young adults was associated with high rates of major side-effects, with about 17 per cent reporting significant fever, eye pain and the need for bed rest.

According to Dr Viera Scheibner (*Vaccination*, New South Wales, 1993), the age of those contracting measles continued to climb well above 10 years and was associated with serious illnesses. Adults and babies below the age of two years, in some cases only a few months old—both populations free from disease before the advent of vaccination—were now contracting measles. By 1984, the establishment blamed these outbreaks on use in the 1960s of what the US Centers for Disease Control and Prevention now termed the "ineffective formalin-inactivated ('killed') measles" vaccine, which had been administered to 600,000 to 900,000 individuals from 1963 to 1967 (Morbidity Mortality Weekly Reports, 4 October 1984). However, other studies demonstrated significant failure among the supposedly improved, live vaccines as well. One outbreak of measles occurred in the junior high schools in Hobbs, New Mexico, where 98 per cent of students had been vaccinated against measles with the live vaccine shortly before the outbreak began (MMWR, 1 February 1985).

Another outbreak of measles occurred in a secondary school population in which more than 99 per cent had records of vaccination with live measles vaccine (New England J Med, 1987, 316: 771-4). One issue of the MMWR (2 September 1988) dealt with 76 measles outbreaks in the US, according to Scheibner. Most of the cases were described as "primary vaccine failures"—which means the vaccine didn't work. During some outbreaks, revaccination with the same vaccines was recommended, even though the scientific evidence demonstrated that revaccination was ineffective.

Scheibner knows of one study on measles revaccination which summarised data published by several authors showing that antibody levels in re-immunised children may fall after several months to very low levels, and that children vaccinated twice may still experience clinically recognisable measles, although in a much milder form. "This state in which a child is immunologically sensitised, but not immune to infection, we shall call 'inadequate immunity'," concluded the authors (Bull WHO, 1984; 62: 315-9).

The PHLS's Dr Begg has echoed the prevailing view that the incidence of measles-vaccine-induced encephalitis is rare, occurring in one in 200,000 children. Symptoms include fever, headache, possible convulsions and behavioural changes. "Most symptoms are mild," he says, "and the children will recover." But, contrary to these statistics, some studies using the same strains report far greater risks. In one published German study, the incidence of reactions to the measles portion of the shot was one neurological complication per 2,500 people vaccinated and one case of temporary encephalitis per 17,650 (Dev of Biol Standards, 1979; 432: 259-64).

"In several studies, the measles vaccine strain has been recovered from the spines of encephalitis victims, showing conclusively that the vaccine caused the encephalitis," says US virologist and immunisation specialist Dr J Anthony Morris.

Wellcome, one of the three original manufacturers of the MMR vaccine in Britain (Merck and Co is the only manufacturer of the live vaccine in the US), reported in *The Data Sheet Compendium*, the British equivalent to *The Physicians' Desk Reference*, that the drug also causes fever, rash, orchitis (inflamed testes), nerve deafness, febrile convulsions, encephalitis, Guillain-Barre syndrome, SSPE and measles which doesn't follow the usual symptoms.

In the study of the SSPE victims cited above, nearly one-third had received a measles vaccine prior to the onset of the illness. "This study cannot confirm or rule out the possibility that the measles vaccine may lead to SSPE on rare occasions," wrote its authors.

New research has made a tentative connection between the measles jab and the sharp rise of Crohn's disease and colitis in children (Lancet, 1994; 343: 105).

The US National Academy of Sciences' IOM report concluded that the measles vaccine can cause death from measles-vaccine-strain infection, thrombocytopenia (a blood condition characterised by a decrease in blood platelets), fatal shock and arthritis. The committee also said it couldn't "rule out" that the vaccine itself could cause cases of SSPE (Stratton, *Vaccines*: 118-86).

Immediately after receiving a measles jab during the nationwide UK campaign in 1994, Sam, a healthy, athletic 12 year old, began losing his sense of co-ordination and falling down. He also began having constant seizures—sometimes 15 an hour. After becoming virtually wheelchair-bound, he was eventually diagnosed as having the fatal condition SSPE. Even though his condition is a known, admittedly rare side effect of the measles shot, his doctors refused to make the link. Instead, they argued that the jab merely set off a latent disease caused by an earlier bout of measles. The problem is, insists his mother, Sam never *had* measles.

The next-generation bombshell

This observation highlights another looming problem, says Scheibner, namely, that generations of girls with this "inadequate immunity" would grow into adults with no placental immunity to pass on to their children, who could then contract measles at an age when babies are normally protected by maternal antibody. This was indeed confirmed by another study, which demonstrated that "hemagglutinin-inhibiting and neutralising antibody titers are lower in women young enough to have been immunised by vaccination than in older women" (J Pediatrics, 1986; 108: 671-76).

Perhaps the most regrettable aspect about striving to eliminate measles by vaccination is that there is no clear need to do so, adds Scheibner. She quotes a large group of Swiss doctors who formed a working committee questioning the Swiss Health Department's US-inspired policy of mass vaccination against measles, mumps and rubella in Switzerland. They quoted measles as an example of a childhood disease with fever and eruptions affecting the organism as a whole. When the process of general inflammation is not correctly handled, the illness may subsequently affect the ears (otitis), the lungs (pneumonia) or the central nervous system, giving rise to the feared complication: encephalitis. "We have lost the common sense and the wisdom that used to prevail in the approach to childhood diseases," they concluded. "Too often, instead of reinforcing the organism's defences, fever and symptoms are relentlessly suppressed. This is not always without consequences. . ."

Rubella

Rubella is a contagious disease which is usually so mild that it often escapes detection. Symptoms, which rarely last more than two or three days, are difficult to distinguish from many chronic childhood problems—runny nose, sore throat and a very slight fever (rarely over 100 degrees). Pink, slightly raised spots may appear on the face and body, and lymph nodes on the back of the head, behind the ears and on the side of the neck may become tender. When contracted by children, it is completely non-threatening and requires no more complicated treatment than letting it run its course.

Rubella can be threatening, however, if a pregnant women contracts the disease during the first three months of pregnancy. If so there is a risk that her baby will be born with congenital rubella syndrome (CRS), which can produce birth defects such as impaired vision and hearing, limb defects, mental retardation and heart malformations.

A couple of years after the UK's mass measles and rubella vaccination campaign of 1994, the number of cases of rubella (German measles) in Scotland was standing at a 13-year high. Research shows that, when children are given preschool jabs as babies' immunity to rubella generally falls off around the age of 11 to 13 years (Ped Infect Dis J, 1996; 15: 687-92). Probably because of this, the emerging cases are mainly among older people—aged between 15 and 34—when the disease is more likely to occur in a pregnant woman and affect her developing foetus. In the latest outbreak, three pregnant women were infected by adults; in all, 169 people were reported to be infected in one four-week cycle, the single highest figure since 1983. About 79 per cent of new cases have been in adult males.

A similar pattern—where the illness suddenly became an adult one—occurred in Finland in 1982 following a mass immunisation programme there (Lancet, 6 April 1996).

Having contracted the disease in childhood a person will have life-long immunity. According to Robert Mendelsohn, before the rubella vaccination was introduced in 1969, nearly 85 per cent of the population was naturally immune to the disease. But today, because most women never get the chance to acquire natural immunity, their risk of contracting rubella during their childbearing years is actually greater.

How effective is it?

Vaccinating against rubella is a pointless exercise. Research quoted by Mendelsohn in his book *But Doctor...* shows that around 25 per cent of those who have the jab show no signs of immunity against the disease within five years following their shots. Other studies put the figure higher: one at 36 per cent, another at 73 per cent. One important study in Australia found that 80 per cent of all army recruits who had been vaccinated against rubella just four months earlier still contracted the disease (Aus J Med Tech, 1973; 4: 26-7).

In epidemics of rubella, a large percentage of victims come from vaccinated or partially vaccinated communities (Am J Dis Child,1972; 124: 27-8). Studies show that the vaccine has a failure rate of around 5 per cent (Med J Aus, 1977; 1: 77). Other studies suggest that the failure rate is higher than reported in vaccine trials (J Roy Soc Med, 1994; 87: 263-4). What is clear is that the protection afforded by vaccination is always inferior to that given by natural infection (Can Med Ass J, 1983; 129: 110-2).

Although the rationale behind rubella vaccination is not to protect children from the disease, but to prevent pregnant women from contacting it and thus giving birth to children with CRS, it is thought that the risk of CRS may be less than we thought. In one study of a partially vaccinated community, 24 women contracted serologically documented prenatal rubella infection. No infant was born with congenital defects and there was no increase in stillbirths or abortions (J Ped, 1974; 84: 474-78). Equally, children with CRS have been reported born to mothers who have been "properly" vaccinated against rubella (Acta Paed, 1994; 83: 674-7).

In spite of the heavy-handed way in which this vaccine is pushed on parents and their children, one study revealed that 90 per cent of obstetricians and more than two-thirds of paediatricians refused to have the rubella vaccine themselves. This was, according to the authors, because the doctors were afraid of "unforeseen vaccine reactions"—a fear engendered by the increased incidence of Guillain-Barre syndrome which followed the mass swine flu immunisation programme in America in 1976 (JAMA, 1981; 245: 711-3).

Side-effects

The rubella vaccine has been found by two separate studies to be the cause of chronic fatigue syndrome. Given to children, the vaccine can linger in their system for years and can be passed to adults through casual contact (Med Hypoth, 1988; 27: 217-8; Clin Ecol, 1989; 7: 51-4). A report by the Committee on Safety in Medicines recently reported three cases of Guillain-Barre syndrome, which causes nerves to inflame, after rubella vaccination. While trumpeting this figure as "reassuring", they conceded the incidence of the disease post-vaccine is under-reported (BMJ, 1996; 312: 1475-6).

In children, skin rash and swollen glands, as well as transient arthritis, follow rubella vaccination (Am J Child Dis, 1969; 218: 218-25) and pain in wrists, hands and knees (JAMA, 1970; 214: 2287-92). Several other studies have shown similar results (J Ped, 1972; 80: 413-17). In fact, the most common adverse reaction to the rubella vaccine is arthritis and related problems such as arthralgia (painful joints) and polyneuritis (pain, numbness or paralysis in the peripheral nerves). Arthritis can be a frequent complication of both natural infection with rubella and immunisation. However, as one group of researchers point out, it is much more frequent in a vaccinated population (Lancet, 1982; *i*: 1323-25). It is thought that as many as 26 per cent of children receiving rubella vaccination develop arthralgia and arthritis (Science, March 26, 1977). The problem is also common in adults who receive the vaccine (Arch Int Med, 1993; 153(19): 2268-74).

A study by the Institutes of Medicine in America concluded that in 13 to 15 per cent of adult women, there was evidence of a causal relationship between the rubella vaccine and acute arthritis (JAMA, 1992; 267: 392-6). The evidence is so clear that both the National Vaccine Injury Compensation Programme and the US Federal Courts have accepted a causal relationship between the vaccine and arthritic conditions (Arth Rheum, 1996; 39: 1529-34). One manufacturer of the triple vaccine concedes in *The Physicians' Desk Reference* that the rubella part of the vaccine causes arthritis in up to 3 per cent of children and in up to 20 per cent of adult women who receive it. "Symptoms [of arthritis] may persist for a matter of months, or on rare occasions, for years," the company reports. Adolescent girls are considered to be at greater risk of joint and limb symptoms.

Dr. Aubrey Tingle, a paediatric immunologist at Children's Hospital in Vancouver, British Columbia, has undertaken major research into this area. According to his own studies, 30 per cent of adults exposed to rubella vaccine suffer arthritis in two to four weeks—ranging from mild aches in the joints to severe crippling. Tingle also found the rubella virus in one-third of adult and child patients with rheumatoid arthritis (MacLean's, 8 February 1982 as reported in Mendelsohn, *But Doctor. . .*: 30).

During the 1994 measles appeal, the Department of Health admitted in written reports to doctors that 11 per cent of first-time recipients of the rubella vaccine will get arthritis.

Nevertheless, this vital fact was omitted in the pamphlet given to patients.

Mumps

Mumps is usually an innocuous disease caused by a virus that attacks one or both salivary (parotid) glands just below and in front of the ears. It's a good example of a nuisance disease being turned into a killer in order to justify the necessity of a vaccine. Two versions of the MMR vaccine, Immravax, manufactured by Merieux, and SmithKline Beecham's Pluserix, were withdrawn in Britain and elsewhere in autumn 1992 because of the risk of the recipient contracting meningitis from the Urabe strain of the mumps portion of the vaccine.

The Japanese government withdrew its own version of the MMR vaccine in April 1993 after discovering a link with meningitis. About a year after withdrawing the vaccination, the authorities there revealed that one in 1,044 vaccinated developed aseptic meningitis. The government also found evidence that the vaccine can bring on mumps, which can be transferred to other children.

When the UK Department of Health (DoH) announced the hasty withdrawal of two of the three brands, the official line circulated to the press about why these drugs were withdrawn, after having been jabbed into millions of 15-months-olds, were allegedly the results of a study showing that the two withdrawn brands had a "negligible" (one in 11,000) risk of causing a "transient" and "mild" (all DoH words, these) cases of meningitis. The third brand, made from a different strain of the mumps virus, supposedly did not pose this risk.

In 1989, when **WDDTY** first interviewed Dr Begg of the UK's Public Health Laboratory Service, which recommended the vaccine in Britain, he assured us that mumps on its own was a very mild illness in children. Mumps, he said, "very rarely" leads to long-term permanent complications such as orchitis (where the disease hits the testicles of adult males, very occasionally causing sterility). "The mumps component had only been added," he said, "to give 'extra value' to the jab."

By 1992, however, when the two versions of the MMR were withdrawn, the British government painted a very different picture, announcing that mumps leads to meningitis in one in 400 cases. Hence, even though the old vaccine was dangerous (and it must have been pretty dangerous to get hauled off the market virtually over night), *it was not as dangerous as catching mumps.*

Whatever the present party line, mumps has never been considered a global killer. The vaccine was only developed because of the rare complications of mumps: orchitis (inflammation of the testes), aseptic meningitis, encephalitis and deafness. Children who get mumps usually suffer a swelling underneath the ear, headache, fever, vomiting and muscle aches. Besides testicles, the female ovaries and breasts can also swell. Symptoms are usually gone in less than a week, although they may last for up to 10 days.

The first mumps vaccine, made from a dead virus, was found to be short-lived and ineffective. Researchers then undertook to develop a weakened live vaccine, grown on hen's eggs and then in chicken embryo cells. Presently, there are three strains: the Jeryl Lynn, Urabe and Leningrad-3 Parkow. The vaccine appears to be slow to take; antibodies don't seem to form for two weeks, and in some it can be delayed for up to six weeks. A fourth strain, the Sofia 6, prepared in guinea-pig kidney primary cell cultures, was introduced in Bulgaria to vaccinate children between one and

12. When it was recognised that the vaccine caused a high level of side-effects, particularly meningitis, it was quickly suspended (Vaccine, 1994; 12: 1251-4).

Indeed, there have been substantial cases where the vaccine has failed and fully vaccinated children have contracted the disease. In one study, six years after the MMR vaccine was put in place, Switzerland suffered an increasing number of mumps cases affecting both vaccinated and unvaccinated children. In an analysis of patients, mumps was confirmed by virus isolation in 88 patients, 72 of whom had received the vaccine, even though antibodies to the mumps virus were detected in 24 out of 27 blood samples gathered in the acute stage of the disease. The study concluded that its data indicates an "insufficient protective efficacy of current mumps vaccines" (Scandinavian J Infectious Diseases, 1996; 28: 235-8). In Britain, the Public Health Laboratory Service studied the antibody levels of 475 children given the MMR vaccine and found that 19 per cent had no evidence of antibodies against mumps (Vaccine, 1995; 13: 799-802). And in Tennessee in America, as with measles, an outbreak of mumps occurred in a highly vaccinated population; there were 68 cases of mumps among 1,116 students, 98 per cent of whom had been vaccinated (J Infectious Disease, 1994; 169: 77-82).

Even the Institute of Medicine admits, in its vaccine review: "Immunity has always been assumed to be long-lasting, but this has never been proven" (Stratton, *Vaccines*: 122). This leads to the question of why we are vaccinating in the first place, since children prevented from getting mumps by a vaccine that almost definitely wears off are more likely to contract the disease when they are older and the disease is likely to be more serious. Although mumps is usually benign in children, it can cause many more problems in adults.

About a third of adolescent or adult males who contract mumps will suffer from orchitis (Moskowitz, *Mothering*).

The mumps portion of the vaccine has been linked with encephalitis, seizures and meningitis. There have also been reports of deafness and orchitis following the mumps vaccine (Stratton), and one case of thrombocytopenia (Lancet, 1970; *i*: 247). Many case reports link simultaneous administration of the mumps and measles vaccine with the onset of insulin-dependent diabetes (Stratton).

German authorities have discovered 27 neurological reactions to the mumps vaccine, including meningitis, febrile convulsions, encephalitis and epilepsy (Lancet, 1989; *ii*: 751). Of all cases of mumps encephalitis over 15 years in America, one-sixth were definitely due to the vaccine (Pediatric Infectious Disease Journal, 1989; 8: 751-5). Research from Canada estimated the risk of vaccine-induced mumps encephalitis was one per 100,000 (Lancet, 1989; *ii*: 1015-16); a Yugoslavian study concluded it was one per 1000 recipients (Pediatric Infectious Disease Journal, 1989; 8: 302-8).

As for meningitis from the mumps vaccine, the British Department of Health's public assurance that the risk is only 1 in 11,000 contradicts the long-known findings published in one of America's leading paediatric journals that the rate varies from 1 in 405 to 1 in 7,000 shots given (Pediatric Infectious Disease Journal, March 1991).

How safe is the MMR vaccine?

In the UK, we are merely told in pamphlets displayed in the doctor's waiting room that the MMR vaccine has been used safely in other countries, particularly the US, for many years, and that it provides "life-long protection against all three infections with a single jab".

What parents who were the target of the 1994 MR

campaign were not told, however, was that a study completed before its launch had shown that children given the MMR jab were three times more likely to suffer convulsions than those who didn't receive it. The study—which was not published until after the end of the campaign—also found that the vaccine caused five times the number of cases of thrombocytopenia purpura, a rare blood disorder over that expected (Lancet, 1995; 345: 567-9).

From July 1990 through April 1994, 5,799 adverse incidents following MMR vaccination were reported to the United States' Vaccine Adverse Events Reporting System. These included 3,063 cases requiring emergency medical treatment, 616 hospitalisations, 309 who didn't recover, 54 children left disabled and 30 deaths.

The US National Vaccine Information Center believes that, because of massive underreporting, these figures represent only 10-15 per cent of the total number of side-effects. This means the true figure could be as high as 60,000 adverse events over the four years since the record-keeping began. In addition, about one in 400 children given the jab will suffer convulsions (Lancet, 1989; ii: 1015-6).

Is there a link between MMR jabs and autism?

In a study published in The Lancet (28 February 1998) the researchers showed a possible link between the vaccine and development of inflammatory bowel disease and autism.

Almost immediately, the government and the medical community rushed out official announcement to deny any association and argued that the findings were sheer coincidence. They maintain that the children received the vaccine when autism would have been first recognised and diagnosed, anyway.

Parents are being urged to continue to give their children

the triple jab, lest a "social tragedy"—by which they mean a measles epidemic—ensue. And now recently, the government is trumpeting the fact that a Finnish study of three million children, also published in The Lancet (2 May 1998), could find no such association between the vaccine and autism. Dr Andrew Wakefield, who led the research, and his colleagues at the Royal Free stand by their findings, advising parents to have the jabs separately until further research is carried out, The government says this type of caution isn't necessary.

Nevertheless, parents have had their confidence in the vaccine badly shaken: according to the Health Education Authority, some 8 per cent of mothers now consider the MMR vaccine more dangerous than measles itself, and one-fifth of mothers now believe the vaccine has considerable side-effects. National vaccine coverage has fallen by 1 to 2 per cent. In the Royal Free study, Dr Wakefield and his colleagues studied 12 children referred to the hospital because of a history of diarrhoea and abdominal pain. (The Royal Free unit specialises in bowel disease.) In all the cases, the children had been developing normally when they suddenly lost their speech and other skills. Eight of the 12 developed autistic symptoms within 14 days of receiving their MMR jab. Five of the children had severe reactions, including fever, rash, delirium or seizures. Most significantly, all 12 had intestinal abnormalities, with 11 showing patchy, chronic inflammation of the colon, seven exhibiting abnormal growths of small nodules of lymphoid tissue, and two suffering from thrush-like ulcers plus huge swellings in their small bowels, according to Wakefield.

Since publishing the study, Wakefield and his team have examined 48 other children with similar behaviour problems which began after the vaccine, 46 of whom exhibited bowel abnormalities similar to those seen in the study subjects. In the view of the Royal Free researchers, the sheer number of children showing up with this peculiar bowel disorder and autistic tendencies which came about after the vaccine was more than could be accounted for by chance.

Wakefield's team hypothesise that in children who are genetically susceptible to autism, the MMR vaccines may damage the intestinal function, which in turn could allow food by-products, called peptides, to pass through the intestinal walls, disrupting brain function and development. Urine tests showed that all the children had marked B12 deficiencies seen in other gastrointestinal disorders. Since B12 is necessary for the normal development of the central nervous system, Wakefield wonders whether the B12 deficiency is a contributory factor in the autistic regression seen in their subjects.

The Royal Free study is not the only disturbing link that has been made between the MMR vaccine and autism. According to Hodge, Jones and Allen, the London-based firm of solicitors which has been contacted by some 1,500 families whose children have been allegedly damaged by the vaccine, a good half of their cases involve children who were developing normally but then became autistic right after vaccination.

Autism is by far the most common side effect reported to Hodge, Jones and Allen, occurring twice as much as any other serious side effect. This is also the case with the 600 families who have registered with JABS, the parent group run by Jackie Fletcher, whose own child Robert was allegedly damaged by the triple jab.

Many of Hodge, Jones and Allen's clients have videotapes of their child's development from birth, month after month, demonstrating normal, healthy development, up until the point of vaccination with MMR, usually at 12 to 15 months.

By that time, the child is usually walking, may have a small vocabulary, and is pointing and interacting with the family. And then suddenly, in every one of these instances, the children have lost their speech and social interaction and made a sudden regression into behaviour patterns which are considered within the autistic spectrum.

These include severe difficulties in communicating and any social interaction with others, withdrawal and repetitive and obsessive movements and patterns of behaviour and sometimes awkward motions.

One mother wrote: "Thomas has gone from being a happy, fun-loving social child to a quiet, introverted and aggressive one. I have a little person who is locked up within himself. And that person within holds the only key to comprehending what makes his world revolve. Our world is one of confusion to Thomas, and outside the home environment, every place, person and activity sparks off anxiety."

Some of Hodge, Jones and Allen's cases involve children up to the age of four, whose normal development and speech is unmistakable up until the point of vaccination. Sarah, whose father is Italian, was bilingual at three-and-a-half, and had a large vocabulary in both languages. Two weeks after her MMR vaccine, she was covered head to waist with the measles rash and suffered a high temperature and drowsiness for a few days.

As soon as the episode was over, she became mute, with autistic traits, as well as bowel disorders and constant diarrhoea. She also developed a blood disorder which has been identified as a side-effect of the MMR vaccine. The fact that children of this age turn autistic after vaccination tends to counter the argument that the onset of autism is coincidental, since autism is diagnosed at a much earlier age.

Another of JABS's members is the mother of triplets, all of

whom were developing normally, a fact that was documented by medical specialists who took extra care with the children because of their multiple-birth status. At 15 months, within three or four days of their MMR jab, all three children suffered a high temperature, drowsiness and loss of appetite. Soon after, they all lost their speech and the ability to make eye contact, and developed behaviour considered typical of autism. One of the children also partially lost his hearing—another known side-effect of the triple jab.

Both the Hodge, Jones and Allen's and JABS's cases indicate that autism is showing up in children under five, suggesting that neurological damage mainly occurs in children when the brain is still developing.

Besides, the anecdotal evidence amassed by the solicitors and JABS, doctors increasingly have been reporting the appearance of what they are calling "atypical autism". This is a disease where the child is developing normally and then suddenly develops autistic behaviour, unlike everyday autism, which is present from birth. Autism is now being reported at an alarming rate. A decade ago, 350 cases of autism were reported every year.

This means there would have been 5,600 cases among British children from one to 16 at any given time. Today, some 10,000 cases have been reported in one British county alone. The National Autistic Society says that nationwide, there are now 518,000 people with autism. This works out to be nearly one in every 100 people in Britain getting a disease which before 1940—the onset of mass vaccination—was virtually unheard of.

A conference paper by a doctor at the University of California's Department of Medicine which studied artistic patients shows the "strong association between immunisation with MMR and the development of autism". The vaccine is not the only one linked to autism. Of five of the children reported to Hodge, Jones and Allen with problems after receiving the *Haemophilus influenzae* type B meningitis vaccine (Hib), two have been diagnosed with autism.

At first glance, the evidence from the Finnish study does appear compelling. The Finnish National Board of Health and the National Public Health Institute launched a vaccination project in 1982 to administer the MMR vaccine to all children at 12-15 months and then at age six. By 1996, three million doses of the vaccine had been given. All adverse effects were supposed to be reported to the Institute. During that time, the study says, 31 children developed gastrointestinal symptoms, with 21 admitted to hospital.

There are a number of important differences between this and the Wakefield research. For one thing, the Wakefield study began with children who'd been diagnosed with an autistic-spectrum disorder and then made the link with the bowel problems. This study, on the other hand, noted only those children with a gastrointestinal problem, among whom none had been diagnosed as autistic. No one was looking for autism particularly as a side effect. More important, this was a passive study, reliant upon doctors to report side-effects. In the Finnish study, many doctors may not have connected certain side-effects, like autism, with the vaccine, or bothered to record them.

Furthermore, there were some serious side-effects, even among the 31 supposedly benign cases of bowel problems. Five of the 31 suffered seizures, three had pneumonia, two lymphadenopathy (enlargement of lymph nodes) and one Guillain-Barre paralysis.

Recently, American researchers from Georgetown University in America offered support for the Wakefield team's autism connection. The researchers have been studying the gut as a "central focus for injury of other target organs" such as the skin, lungs and gastrointestinal tract (Lancet, 1998; 352: 234-5).

Whether or not the autism link proves right, there is no doubt that vaccines, particularly the MMR, which contains three live vaccines, can cause subtle damage to the nervous system and the brain. Scientists accept that vaccination can cause encephalitis in children.

Encephalitis is an inflammation of the brain, often referred to as meningitis, causing a bulging and red fontanel in infants. In this circumstance, the child may seem to recover completely, but he may actually have suffered some long-term damage. A follow-up study in the British Medical Journal in 1993 of the National Childhood Encephalopathy Study concluded that children who had suffered an acute reaction from the whooping cough vaccine suffered from a permanent neurological disability later in life.

Medical historian Dr Harris Coulter studied an epidemic of encephalitis in the 1920s and 1930s, which affected 20 to 30 million people world-wide.

It accounted for a couple of million deaths, with an equivalent number of survivors suffering from serious disabilities. Coulter found that the types of consequences after an epidemic of encephalitis were identical to what we call today "minimal" brain damage and seizure disorders.

In many instances—whether epilepsy, autism or minimal brain damage—says Dr Coulter, what "bent the twig" is an attack of encephalitis in infancy caused in most cases by routine vaccination.

How prevalent is encephalitis after vaccination? Doctors recognise this happens, but insist it occurs only once in every 100,000 cases. In Dr Coulter's view, an encephalitic reaction happens about one in every five children. When the MMR was introduced in this country, the PHLS tested it on many thousands of children. In that study, convulsions occurred in one in every 400 children (Lancet, 1989; *ii*: 1015-6).

This incidence was deemed by the PHLS to be acceptable, as, in their view, all these babies and toddlers recovered completely—even though no long-term studies were ever done to see if they were minimally brain damaged or had learning difficulties.

The most definitive and the largest study of vaccines to date, conducted by the US CDC, used database technology to monitor the progress of 500,000 children across the US, tapping into computerised records of health maintenance organisations and public insurance schemes.

In this way, the CDC was able to pull together virtually every piece of research and data into adverse reactions to the two triple vaccines. They identified 34 major side-effects to the jabs, ranging from asthma, blood disorders, infectious diseases, diabetes and neurological disorders, including meningitis, polio and hearing loss. But it was the incidence of seizure that leaped off the graph. The rate of seizure increased three times above the norm within the first day of a child receiving the DPT (diphtheria-pertussis-tetanus) shot, and the rate rose 2.7 times within four to seven days of a child being given the MMR shot, increasing to 3.3 times within eight to 14 days (Pediatrics, 1997; 99: 765-73).

Seizure, which covers epilepsy, convulsions and fainting, is already one of the most common childhood conditions, affecting an estimated one in 20 children, or 5 per cent. This could reflect the influence of vaccinations, or the CDC's findings could mean that vaccines will further increase the seizure rate to nearly 15 per cent, or one in every six children—close to Dr Coulter's figures.

The effects of the DPT shot were immediate, causing seizures to increase three times the norm within 24 hours of the jab being given, but then falling off rapidly to just 0.06 times the norm after the first day. The MMR vaccine, however, had a far slower effect, only reaching its most dangerous period within eight days to two weeks after the jab was administered. The seizures were often serious, the CDC reported, with a quarter of all cases being treated in hospital.

The findings of Britain's PHLS are nearly identical. The PHLS Statistic Unit also found that the MMR jab increased seizure risk three times, and that two-thirds of the cases of seizures were due to the measles component alone (Lancet, 1995; 345: 567-9). The CDC is carrying out further research to determine whether the seizures are caused by the individual vaccines, or whether the problem is caused by so many vaccines being given at the same time.

But measles doesn't strike and kill randomly. When vitamin A levels are low, the outer layer of our mucous membranes become scaly and the turnover of cells decreases. The measles virus infects and damages these tissues throughout the body. Blood concentrations of vitamin A, even in the well-nourished child, may decrease to levels normally associated with malnourished children. During measles, children with marginal liver stores of vitamin A may develop an acute vitamin A deficiency, resulting in eye damage and possibly increased deaths from respiratory disease and diarrhoea. One study showed that even children with only a mild vitamin A deficiency were more at risk (Lancet, 1986; *i*: 1169-73). This is why measles claims the lives of so many malnourished children in Third World countries. However, giving vitamin A to children with measles can lessen the complications or chances of dying from the disease—even among African children (New Eng J of

Med, 1990; 323: 160-4). In central Tanzania, death rates were reduced by seven times among those children given vitamin A, particularly in children under two (BMJ, 1987; 294: 294-6).

In another study in New York in 1992, New York researchers measured vitamin A levels in 89 New York children younger than two years with measles. Those with lower levels of vitamin A were more likely to have fever of 40 degrees or higher and to be hospitalised (Am J Dis Child, 1992; 146: 182-6).

A strange hysteria seems to have subsumed officialdom which places blanket coverage of vaccination and low incidence of disease above anything else, including vaccine safety or even necessity. As Dr Richard Nicolson points out: "The fact that people don't trust the vaccine sums up the mess you get into when you don't tell the truth from the start. The government has to change its approach to give people an honest picture of what we do and do not know, rather than continuing to offer a load of platitudinous and comforting statements that no longer make a great deal of scientific sense. There are remarkably few interventions in medicine that don't carry some risk, so to say that vaccines are perfectly safe is highly unlikely."

SIDE-EFFECTS OF THE MMR VACCINE

Measles portion:
A US National Academy of Sciences study concluded that the measles vaccine can cause death from measles-vaccine-strain infection, thrombocytopenia (a blood condition characterised by a decrease in blood platelets), fatal shock and arthritis. The committee also said it couldn't "rule out" that the vaccine itself could cause SSPE, a fatal disease (Stratton, Adverse Events: 118-86).

Rubella portion:
Chronic fatigue syndrome (Med Hypoth, 1988; 27: 217-8; Clin Ecol, 1989; 7: 51-4), Guillain-Barre syndrome (BMJ, 1996; 312: 1475-6) and transient arthritis (Am J Child Dis, 1969; 218: 218-25) and pain in wrists, hands, and knees (JAMA, 1970; 2287-92). As many as 26 per cent of children receiving rubella vaccination develop arthralgia and arthritis (Science, 26 March 1977; Health Freedom New, July/Aug 1984). The Institutes of Medicine concluded that in 13 to 15 per cent of adult women there was evidence of a causal relationship between the rubella vaccine and acute arthritis (JAMA, 1992; 267: 392-6).

Mumps portion:
Encephalitis, seizure and meningitis. There have also been reports of deafness and orchitis following the mumps vaccine (Stratton) and one case of thrombocytopenia (Lancet, 1970; *i*: 247). Many case reports link simultaneous administration of the mumps and measles vaccine with the onset of insulin-dependent diabetes (Stratton).

Chapter six

HIB MENINGITIS

Perhaps the worst example of vaccine double-think concerns the *Haemophilus influenzae* type b (or Hib, for short) vaccine, which was first licensed in the US in 1985 and released in Britain in October 1992. This is supposed to combat the most common cause of meningitis in children under five—even though many forms have never worked on those most at risk.

Hib meningitis causes upper respiratory and ear infections, pneumonia and spinal cord inflammation. The peak attack age in a child is between six and 12 months, and three-quarters of all cases occur in children under two (Miller, *Vaccines*).

This form of bacterial meningitis, caused by *Haemophilus influenzae* type b, mainly strikes at pre-school children, with the peak incidence occurring between six and 15 months of age. When the vaccine was introduced, the estimates were that some 60 out of every 100,000 children would contract Hib-caused meningitis; of those, between three and 6.5 per cent would die and 14 per cent have continuing problems, such as deafness or seizures. In the UK, precise records haven't been kept, although we do know that Hib caused about 20 deaths in children per year.

Certain groups—notably Alaskan and Native American children—are at higher risk, contracting the disease at rates 10 to 50 times higher than the population at large. Both groups are thought to be predisposed to the disease because of genetic factors or malnutrition.

Current child care practices, specifically our tendency to institutionalise children too early, have given rise to epidemics of this form of meningitis among well-nourished white populations. Dr Robert Mendelsohn and his editor Vera Chatz were the first to warn of the dangers of warehousing large groups of non-toilet-trained babies. Mendelsohn's suspicions were soon backed up by various studies in the medical literature, showing that day-care facilities are suffering an epidemic of Hib-caused meningitis.

In the June 1986 supplement of Pediatrics, cited by Mendelsohn in *But Doctor. . . About that Shot*, researchers examining eight day-care centres found that the attack rate of this type of meningitis was 1,100 cases per 100,000—almost double that of the US child population at large. A more recent study by the American Journal of Public Health (1990: 80) concluded that centres most at risk included those where workers used towels or handkerchiefs to wipe children's noses, or allowed in children who had diarrhoea or weren't toilet trained.

Ironically, the worst places were those that were commercial, rather than those staffed by volunteers.

The first vaccine introduced in America in 1985 was a polysaccharide, used in children over 15 months old, largely after one Finnish trial had encouraging results. The vaccine soon began to lose credibility after doctors reported that cases of meningitis were showing up in children right after they had been vaccinated. One Minnesota study showed that the shot increased their risk fivefold of contracting the disease. The drug also didn't work on children less than 18 months—the very population most at risk (Mendelsohn, *But Doctor. . .*: 87).

In its US-government sponsored report, the National Academy of Sciences Institute of Medicine confirmed that the Hib vaccine can cause Hib meningitis (Stratton, *Vaccines*).

And in another study, where 55 children went on to develop Hib-caused meningitis, not only did the vaccine not have any protective effect (particularly since three children died and six had neurological complications), but the researchers concluded that the vaccine *increased* susceptibility to these complications (our italics).

After 1992, when a study of 10 million children by the US Centers for Disease Control showed that this version of the vaccine only protected two-thirds of children, medicine junked the polysaccharide version of the vaccine as hopelessly unreliable (Lancet, 1991; 338: 395-8).

Once the polysaccharide vaccine was discredited, several companies came up with a conjugate vaccine (ie, one that would marry the Hib portion with the tried and tested diphtheria vaccine (PRP-D); the diphtheria-pertussis-tetanus vaccine (PRP-DPT); or even the *Neisseria meningitidis* group b outer membrane protein complex (PRP-OMPC).

The idea behind all this initialled gobbledygook was that attaching the two vaccines on to a substance known to produce antibodies would prompt the body to come up with an antibody to the Hib bug as well.

Lederle Laboratories has released HibTITER and Connaught ProHIBit. Lederle's drug was licensed in November 1990 to be given to American children at two, four and six months of age—the same time as the polio and DPT vaccines. The OMPC version even seemed to work on Navajo infants (New Eng J Med, 1991; 324: 1767-72).

In 1993, the US FDA approved Tetramune, a combination of the DTP vaccine and Hib vaccine, for use on babies and children between two months and five years. Besides supposedly kickstarting the Hib vaccine into working better, this combination would also reduce from eight to four the number of shots US children have to get. Or so the theory went. Nevertheless, tests on nearly 7,000 children showed that the all-in-one variety produced no significant difference in antibody response than the separate shots (J Am Med Assoc, 1993; 269: 2491).

Despite the medical professions belief that it has finally cracked the problem, studies are popping up here and there with less than ideal results. One published in The Lancet (1991; 338: 395-8) found that nine children with Hib-caused meningitis had received the diphtheria conjugate vaccine at least two weeks before they'd contracted the disease. The study put the protective effect of the PRP-D vaccine at 74 per cent—only slightly more than the regular Hib vaccine, which offers an estimated 64 per cent protection.

In fact, the vaccine only gave about 35 per cent protection for the high-risk Alaskan infants, even after three doses.

America also had problems with bad batches of the vaccine, which didn't take. Some batches of one of the leading brands of Hib vaccine in the US have been shown to have lower than expected immunogenicity. The faulty batches comprised some 366,000 doses—or 2 per cent of Hib conjugate vaccine released in the US since January 1990.

Even PRP-OMPC, the most successful conjugate, has had its problems. A Los Angeles' study (AJDC, 1991; 145: 742) showed that the more vaccine a child received, the lower his antibody response. A 1995 study in Pittsburgh, Pennsylvania found that 52 per cent of cases of Hib meningitis represented vaccine failures—nine with the polysaccharide vaccine and two with the conjugate vaccine (Pediatrics, 1995; 96: 424-7).

The Pediatric Infectious Disease Journal (1992; 18: 6) has made a connection between the increasing prevalence of penicillin-resistant pneumococcal meningitis and universal Hib vaccination.

In the UK, Hib meningitis has been all but eliminated. In

both 1994 and 1995, only one case a year was reported in Oxford, where 63 cases were previously reported every year. Similarly, just eight cases of Hib in children under the age of five from five other regions were seen in the nine months from October 1994, compared to 270 and 269 cases in similar periods in 1990 and 1991. So successful has been the campaign, say the experts, that no booster shot is needed when the child is aged two. According to the UK's Public Health Laboratory Service, the laurel wreath should go to an effective vaccination programme. Unfortunately, there is one niggling statistic that deserves to be heard. Of the 164 cases reported in the year from October 1992, 43 were true vaccine failures and, of these, 31 had the prescribed three shots. So is the vaccine really so effective after all—or is medicine trying to take credit for a cyclical downturn in a disease, as other experts (Lancet, 1997: 349: 1197-1201) have suggested?

More evidence casting doubt on the usefulness of vaccination against meningitis has emerged in research by the Haemophilus Influenzae Study Group (JAMA, 1993; 269: 227-31; also 269: 264-6). In a study generally extolling the virtues of the Hib vaccination in cutting the number of meningitis cases, the group concedes that a substantial fall also occurred in children who hadn't been vaccinated—down from 99.3 per 100,000 in 1989 to 68.5 per 100,000 in 1990.

This particular drop, they add, is consistent with previously identified cyclic variation in meningococcal disease incidence—that is, the disease reaches a peak and then goes into decline over a number of subsequent years. Although the reason for this cyclical variation is not known, it raises the possibility that the observed variation in meningococcal disease rates may not represent an effect of changes in medical therapy or diagnosis. That's a round-about way of saying the vaccine may have had no effect.

Chapter seven

TUBERCULOSIS

Tuberculosis, caused by the *Mycobacterium tuberculosis* bacteria, primarily attacks the lungs but also can affect other organs. The early symptoms include listlessness, vague chest pain, inflammation of the membranes around the lungs, loss of appetite, fever and weight loss. Later, night sweats, bleeding in the lungs, coughing up sputum and shortness of breath develop, particularly as small groups of cells (tubercles) in the lungs surround the pathogens, eventually enlarging and leaving dead tissue in the cavities of the lungs. Rare complications include tuberculous meningitis, and periotonitis (which causes severe abdominal pains and vomiting), tuberculous bones and joints, and tuberculosis of the kidneys.

Children with primary tuberculosis are especially prone to rapid and bodywide infection, but recover quickly. Tuberculosis sometimes causes disorders of the lymph glands. Unless the strain is resistant, tuberculosis can be treated with antibiotics.

The BCG (bacille Calmette-Guerin) vaccine, named after the strain of bacteria from which it derives, was routinely offered to British school children aged between 10 and 14. This vaccine was administered to all British and American children in the 1950s and 1960s.

The DoH expected that the national BCG school programme would no longer be needed by 1996, once the incidence of TB continued to decline, from 117,000 cases and 50,000 deaths in 1913 to 6,000 cases per year today. However, TB has made a comeback in overcrowded neighbourhoods of British inner cities, or among certain Asian populations, and many TB strains have emerged that are resistant to antibiotics.

The number of reported cases has slightly increased, half occurring among children of Asians and other immigrants and a high percentage in inner cities such as Leeds or the East End of London.

The joint committee was also stymied over the possible role of HIV in what appeared to be the sudden rallying of the tuberculosis germ, since these same groups also suffer a high incidence of HIV and AIDS. So, erring on the side of caution, the committee recommended that the schools' BCG programme be continued for another five years.

Besides school children, the Department of Health recommends that BCG be given at birth to Asian and other immigrant families with high TB rates; those who live in or travel to areas of high risk; those in contact with active TB; those with a family history of TB in the past five years; and children living in crowded conditions in inner cities. In other words, to protect a minority at high risk (who would mostly be protected by the shot at birth), the department is needlessly exposing a majority, who has almost no chance of contracting the disease, to the vaccine.

If you haven't been immunised against the disease and plan to stay for more than a month in Asia, Africa, Central or South America, the DoH also recommends that you get the BCG vaccine, particularly if you are going to be living or working alongside indigenous populations, or if you are visiting your country of origin. But for all this vigilance, the BCG vaccine isn't working. TB is rampant in tropical countries where vaccination programmes have been intensive, making the World Health Organization's ambition of a TB-free world by the Year 2000 a forlorn hope.

The vaccine is just 22 per cent effective in Kenya, and 20 per cent effective in some areas of India. Its protection over time also seems to wear off. In one trial in southern India, its efficacy fell from 80 per cent to zero in 20 years, reports Professor P Fine at the London School of Hygiene and Tropical Medicine, in a special analysis for The Lancet.

Overall effectiveness ranges from zero to 80 per cent around the world, with the variation due possibly to strain variations, genetic or nutritional differences, and to environmental influences (Lancet, 1995; 346: 1339-45). One theory maintains that high latitude makes the vaccine more efficient, possibly accounting for 41 per cent of variations.

Schools testing—is it accurate?

The British Medical Journal (1992; 302: 495-8) showed that 92 per cent of districts were carrying out routine BCG immunisation. The Heaf test is used by 95 per cent of the school districts interviewed to measure tuberculin sensitivity. Unlike most sensitivity tests, a negative result is supposed to mean that the child does not carry antibodies to the tubercle bacillus. However, the test is notoriously inaccurate; even the American Academy of Pediatrics warns its members that the test carries the possibility of false negatives and false positives. Dr Robert Mendelsohn used to say that the potential dangers of the test, with its threat of dangerous vaccination, were more dangerous than the threat of the disease.

Furthermore, no one is really sure what a positive test really means. It could mean that someone is immune to tuberculosis, or prior infection, or it could mean that someone is simply allergic or sensitive to the test.

In the BMJ study, most districts agreed on what to do with a 0 grade, which showed very little reaction (recommend immunisation) or a Grade 3 or 4, which indicated a pronounced reaction (refer to a chest clinic for special evaluation before going ahead with the shot).

The disparity occurred with those scoring grade 2. One-third of the districts recommended no action (ie, no immunisation) and two-thirds, referral to a chest clinic for special examination before the shot is administered. Only a single district recommended immunisation at this level of sensitivity to the test. Some 10 per cent of unvaccinated children in the study scored grade 2 or higher on the test. Medical Monitor goes as far as to label the tuberculin tests "inaccurate". A positive tuberculin test, it says, doesn't always imply protection against the disease.

Other problems

Besides the lack of agreement about which groups should or should not receive the shot, there are a host of other problems with this live vaccine. For one thing, substantial doubts exist about its effectiveness. Medical Monitor (5 June 1992) reported that "in 10 randomised controlled trials from around the world since the 1930s, the protective efficacy of BCG vaccination has ranged from 0 to 80 per cent, although higher rates are reported with use [among newborns]".

On average, it concludes, the shot only protects about 65 per cent of exposed children against pulmonary disease. In Sweden, four in every 100,000 one-year-olds suffered severe immunodeficiency syndrome (Acta Paed, 1993; 82: 1043-52). The article also admits that BCG vaccination can only limit the multiplication and spread of the tubercle bacteria; it cannot prevent infection in people exposed to the germ: "It can cause disseminated TB in immunosuppressed individuals, including children, and local ulceration and osteitis [inflammation and wasting away of bone] appear to be more common with its use in [babies]," said the Monitor.

This highlights the potential of the vaccine to cause TB, particularly in immune-compromised recipients. One study of 5,000 reports about the vaccine identified 28 cases of TB following the BCG vaccine. Twenty-four of the recipients had immune system problems; 71 per cent of the patients were under two, and the same percentage died from the disease. Most patients came from developed countries. The study also found that cases of TB occur after revaccination of people who were anergic—that is, did not produce an immunological response—after being given an initial dose of BCG vaccine (Clin Infectious Diseases, 1997; 24: 1139-46).

Other side effects include lymphadenitis and generalised lymphadenopathy (that is, inflammation or disease of the lymphatic system, the complex network in the body that maintains the fluid environment and which is vital to the immune system). The complication rate is 0.3 to 0.6 per cent. In other words, between three and six of every 1,000 children will suffer a reaction from the vaccine.

A further unexpected "side effect" of this vaccine has been found. The Lancet (1992; 339: 636-9) carried a study of 83,000 individuals in Malawi who'd been vaccinated with BCG and found that about half were protected against leprosy but could find "no statistically significant protection by BCG against tuberculosis. These findings add to the evidence that BCG vaccines afford greater protection against leprosy than against tuberculosis," said the study. In Kenya, where TB protection is just 22 per cent, the vaccine offers 81 per cent protection against leprosy (Lancet, 1995; 346: 1339-45).

Another study (Lancet, August 15, 1992) from University

Teaching Hospital in Zambia argued convincingly that BCG vaccine given to infants born to HIV mothers actually causes the disease, since the hosts are immunocompromised.

There is ample evidence that this vaccine, as many others, particularly those administered live, may harm natural immunity, especially in a child with a weakened immune system. Increasingly, many doctors believe that ME could be caused by drugs like the BCG vaccine, by in some way interfering with the immune system.

Chapter eight

FLU VACCINE

The safety and efficacy of the flu vaccine is debatable, especially since the strains covered by one year's vaccine rarely correspond to the strains causing the flu at that time. The flu virus is genetically complex—a kind of microbial chameleon which has thrived over the millennia by rigorously adhering to a single maxim: adapt or die.

By examining the history of influenza epidemics of the eighteenth and nineteenth centuries, scientists have been able to recognise certain patterns. The virus seems to be able to change itself often enough so that, at least once in every human generation, a significantly new strain appears which can elude the human immune system. Most epidemiologists are frankly dumbstruck by the virus's ability to outsmart our collective human intelligence.

Predicting a flu epidemic is rather like predicting the weather. All sorts of things outside of human control can conspire against the accuracy of the prediction. This was aptly illustrated in 1976 when American scientists were predicting a swine-flu epidemic which would equal the great flu pandemic of 1918. In fact, in 1976, pneumonia and influenza related deaths were at their lowest for years (Morbid Mortal Weekly Report, 1976; 25: 391-2) and, to the chagrin of a government which spent millions preparing a vaccine, the dreaded swine flu never did materialise.

Vaccines may, at best, be 75 per cent effective in protecting the elderly and other high-risk people (Drugs & Aging, 1995; 6: 368-87). Some studies indicate that as many as 30-40 per cent of elderly people do not respond to influenza vaccination (Hum Immunol, 1994; 40: 202-9).

A Leicester-based study (BMJ, April 10, 1993) found that almost a third of those who received a flu jab didn't need it. They had none of the underlying factors—chronic cardiovascular, pulmonary or renal disease, or diabetes— which would supposedly place them at greater risk.

Of those who might really find a jab useful, less than half end up being immunised. For instance, 90 per cent of influenza-related deaths occur among those over age 65. But, according to the 1991 National Health Interview Survey, during the preceding year only 41 per cent of those age 65 or over received the influenza vaccine (Morbid Mortal Weekly Report, 1993; 42: 768-70). Although all flu vaccines are allowed to be given to infants in the US, only one, Fluzone, is approved for babies in the UK (all other ones are for adults and children over four). Fluzone is made by Squibb-Connaught in the US. The vaccine is supposed to be used for children at high risk—those with chronic lung, heart, kidney and endocrine diseases, and also those exposed to drugs that suppress the immune system. But it gives only short-term protection and supposedly must be repeated every season.

It can be difficult to motivate the general population, who are less at risk, to accept the flu vaccine. For example, from 1968 to 1974 the best turn-out for flu immunisation in the US was in 1968 during the Hong Kong flu epidemic, when a mere 10.7 per cent of the population got their shots, despite the epidemic's severity. By 1974, US flu vaccination rates had plummeted to 8 per cent of the general population and a poor 17.4 per cent among the elderly who were considered at a special risk. In the UK, fewer than 12 per cent of NHS physicians promoted the use of the flu vaccine to elderly or hospitalised patients. More revealing is that less than 6 per cent of London nurses agreed to have themselves vaccinated against flu in any given year from 1968 to 1975 (*Influenza: Viruses, Vaccines and Strategy*, ed Philip Selby, New York: Academic Press, 1976). Both Parke Davis, which manufactures Fluogen, and Wyeth-Ayerst, which produces Influenza Virus Vaccine, have to formulate their products differently each season, in accordance with the Office of Biologics of the Food and Drug Administration regulations, depending on which flu is currently making the rounds.

It is thought that influenza viruses are carried around the world in avian species, specifically ducks and other wild birds. These viruses are capable of causing cross-species epidemics not just in humans but in other animals like chickens or seals, such as those who died off around the US and the UK in the 1980s (*Emerging Viruses*, Oxford University Press, 1993).

Historical, economic and political factors affect vaccination practices and policies internationally, perhaps more than health concerns. A comparative review of flu vaccine use in 18 developed countries showed that in countries where national or social health insurance was in place, vaccine use was higher (Vaccine, 1995; 13: 623-7). In the period from 1980 to 1993, however, the use of vaccines in the US more than doubled to 159 doses per 1,000 individuals. This may, as one review comments, be more of a reflection of the entrepreneurial nature of American medical practice than of individual or public-sector concern about the ravages of the flu (Clin Infec Dis, 1995; 20: 1317-6).

Does the vaccine work?

Studies into the efficiency of the flu vaccine show conflicting results (Gerontol, 1995; 41: 3-10). There is a question mark hanging over the effectiveness of the inactivated viruses used in flu vaccines and whether they can actually provide complete protection (Int Arch Allergy Immunol, 1995; 108: 318-20). And even if immune responses are stimulated (as confirmed by blood samples), there is doubt as to whether this response decreases the incidence of influenza (Vaccine, 1994; 12: 1185-9).

Mistakes are also possible in the manufacture of flu vaccines, which can render them useless. In 1976, when the panic was on about swine flu, Parke-Davis had to recall two million doses of vaccine against the wrong flu strain (Morbid Mortal Weekly Report, 1976, 25: 221-7). More recently, Parke-Davis recalled 11 lots of Fluogen vaccine when they were found to be substandard. Elderly nursing-home residents who took the substandard vaccine had lower antibody responses to influenza (Morbid Mortal Weekly Report, 1996; 45: 1100-2).

As the late Dr Robert Mendelsohn reported in *But Doctor . . . About That Shot*, a 1985 Vaccines and Related Biological Products Advisory Committee of the Centers for Disease Control studied nursing-home patients in seven US states given flu shots over four successive seasons. Their conclusion: the drug afforded no protection against influenza B.

Side-effects

The flu vaccine has been associated with an increased incidence of encephalitis. A UK manufacturer of the vaccine, Servier, reports in the Data Sheet Compendium about Fluvirin, its earlier drug (which was only for patients older than four years), that "cases of encephalomyelitis and neuritis have been reported rarely". Besides these side effects, the drug has also caused anaphylactic shock, plus "headache, pyrexia [fever], and a feeling of malaise". In one Spanish study, nearly 10 per cent of recipients of the flu vaccine had one or more symptoms—fever, malaise and conditions requiring confinement in bed—not unlike the flu itself! (Medicina Clinica, 1996; 106: 11-4)

In 1976, when the US government was pushing its citizens to accept a vaccination to protect against swine flu, the number of cases of Guillain-Barre syndrome shot up. Guillain-Barre syndrome causes weakness, respiratory failure and paralysis. Its cause is unknown and there is no cure. Some people die from it, others recover completely and there is no way to tell how or why this happens.

The normal rate for Guillain-Barre was one out of every million people per year. But among swine-flu-vaccine recipients the attack rate was about 10 times greater, at one case in every 100,000 Americans (Am J Epidemiol, 1979; 110: 105-23). By 1993, the US government had paid out nearly $93 million of taxpayers' money to victims of the swine-flu jab.

More recently, there is new evidence that the flu vaccine can cause pulmonary complications and exacerbate asthma. In one double-blind, placebo-controlled study, carried out at several hospitals in England, roughly one in 12 patients—8 per cent—experienced a trigger of asthma from the flu vaccine (Lancet, 1998; 351: 326-31). One **WDDTY** reader, a medical homoeopath, says that a patient of hers developed periodic asthma-like attacks requiring hospitalisation immediately following her flu jab—a condition finally cured with homoeopathy.

The flu vaccine has also been linked with optic neuritis and permanent blindness (Am J Ophthalmology, 1997; 124: 703-4; J Neuro-Ophthalmology, 1998, 18: 56-9); vasculitis and joint problems (J Rheumatology, 1997; 24: 1198-202); reversible paralysis (Nederlands Tijd voor Geneeskunde,

1995; 139: 2152-4); and myelopathy (Muscle & Nerve, 1995; 18; 1199-201).

Individuals who are at greatest risk from the flu may also be at greater risk from the flu jab. For instance, in HIV positive individuals, levels of HIV-1 have been reported to increase in peripheral blood after the jab (Clin Eper Immunol, 1996; 104(2): 203-7; Ped Infec Dis J, 1996; 15(3): 197-203).

The flu vaccine activates T-cell response, and it is this which can put a strain on the systems of HIV-positive individuals. It can also create problems for those who are not HIV positive. In 1991, the US blood centres reported an unusual increase in donations that tested falsely reactive for antibodies to two or more (multiple false positive) of three different viruses: HIV-1, human T-cell lymphotrophic virus type I (HTLV-I) and hepatitis C. Many of these donations were from people who had recently received the 1991-1992 influenza vaccine (JAMA, April 28, 1993; Am J Epidemiol, 1995; 141: 1089-96). False positive results are likely for three to six months after receiving the jab.

This was perhaps the most public effect seen of flu vaccines, but there have been other, smaller reports of side effects of flu vaccination. One 61-year-old women experienced bilateral optic neuritis (inflamed nerves in both eyes) and loss of vision following a influenza vaccination (J Neuro Opthamol, 1996; 16: 182-4). In another case, a patient experienced acute transverse myelitis (inflammation of the spine) after a flu shot (J Neuroimaging, 1996; 6: 248-50).

Similarly, in another instance a healthy woman aged 56 was vaccinated for the second year in succession against influenza. Three days afterwards, she developed a strange sensation in her legs and lower abdomen, and experienced difficulty urinating and defecating. A diagnosis of myelopathy (a spinal disease) was made. It took six months for her neurological functions to return to normal (Nederlands Tijdschrift voor Geneeskunde, 1995; 139: 2152-4).

Three other patients developed systemic vasculitis (inflammation of the blood vessels) following a flu jab (J Rheum, 1993; 20(8): 1429-31).

WDDTY readers have also expressed their doubts about the safety of flu jabs. One reader in London wrote that it took his elderly uncle, who was in his 80s, six weeks to recover from a jab. His mother, also in her 80s was ill for about the same length of time and was left with a lingering cough. Several other members of his family and their friends, living in London, Leeds and York, all aged 60 plus, experienced similar symptoms, leaving him to wonder whether the flu jab actually causes flu, rather than prevents it.

THE VACCINATION BIBLE

Chapter nine

HEPATITIS B

Hepatitis B is a liver disease caused by a virus. It is a more deadly form of hepatitis, and unlike hepatitis A, it is spread through the passage of body fluids. However, as there are usually less than 50 cases contracted abroad every year in the UK, this is not a serious threat.

In other parts of the world, there is a moderate risk of HB infection, with 2–7 per cent of the population being HB carriers. Of the reported cases, approximately 1.4 per cent are fatal.

It used to be a disease mainly confined to intravenous drug users and gay men. However, now that it appears regularly in donated blood, medicine has been keen to vaccinate against it. The World Health Assembly has considered a recommendation that hepatitis B (HB) vaccination be included in the routine vaccination schedule for babies or children all over the world, regardless of whether they are at high risk of contracting the disease, which can damage the liver and kill one in five carriers.

America followed the lead of 33 countries, which have national policies on HB shots. However, American doctors do not support the government recommendations. In a survey in North Carolina, only a third of paediatricians and a fifth of family doctors supported the new guidelines.

In Italy, the jab is compulsory; in the US, the HB shot is included in the schedules for infants; in the UK, the Health

Secretary once considered whether to embark on what would become upon the largest scheme of its kind since the mass smallpox immunisation programme of the 1960s, recommending that 12-year-olds—on the brink of sexual activity—be vaccinated against what is primarily a sexually transmitted disease.

In 1979, when a hepatitis vaccine was released on the market, the strategy in the UK and the US was to identify and vaccinate high-risk groups, including intravenous drug abusers, the sexually promiscuous, and health care workers who handle bodily fluids and blood. Despite these efforts, hepatitis cases have risen by a third between 1979 and 1989. Since the exact source of the disease is unknown, the authorities wonder whether we should nip it in the earliest possible bud—in infants. This means they believe we should exploit the immune systems of children to prevent what is primarily a sexually transmitted disease from spreading among adults.

The AIDS issue

What no one is talking about is how the old vaccine got made. No vaccine production is very pretty, but this is one of the few which used to be derived from human blood—specifically, the blood products of homosexual men who have had hepatitis.

The vaccine was replaced in the early 1990s by a genetically engineered, or "recombinant", version of the vaccine, which is grown on yeast cells. However, the earlier plasma-derived vaccine was never withdrawn, and even those drug companies which stopped producing the blood-derived product kept selling it until it was used up. So until very recently, anyone receiving the vaccine could have received a blood-based product.

The New York Blood Center addressed this issue by

studying hundreds of cases in low- and high-risk populations receiving the vaccine. Their conclusion: no one is at a higher risk of developing HIV infections from the hepatitis B vaccine. Those in favour of the vaccine argue that the process that kills the hepatitis virus also kills any other viruses lurking about. But remember, at the moment, many high-level scientists, including the co-discoverer of the AIDS virus, are questioning the single-virus theory of AIDS. It's entirely possible that a number of "co-factors" in the blood causing or contributing to AIDS which we don't currently understand may not be killed by this process. The Health Secretary in his announcement called this vaccine "perfectly safe". Until we understand what causes AIDS, no one can make that statement with certainty.

The AIDS question may be why doctors, nurses and other "high risk" health care workers have avoided the old vaccine like the plague. In 1992, a questionnaire was sent to 595 GPs. Although most of them wrote that all GPs should be vaccinated against hepatitis B, only about half had the shot themselves (US Medicine, April 1983).

Another problem with the HB shot is that patients vaccinated for hepatitis B sometimes give a false positive reading on an HIV test (Lancet, 1992; 339: 1060).

In 1988, New Zealand was one of the first countries to adopt a universal programme of HB vaccination of newborn babies. The plan was to inoculate babies of less infectious mothers throughout the country and all the babies of seven districts. On 4 May 1992, noted vaccine critic Dr Anthony Morris presented a report to the Vaccine Safety Committee, Institute of Medicine, of the National Academy of Sciences in Washington, DC. Dr Morris and Hilary Butler, of the Immunisation Awareness Society in Tuakau, in Auckland, New Zealand, had compiled a report on the experience of the

New Zealand authorities in seven districts of the country.

Morris and Butler's report, "The Nature and Frequency of Adverse Reactions Following the Hepatitis B Vaccine Injection in Children in New Zealand from 1985-88", is the first to track the reported side effects of the HB vaccine in one country over three years, and also the first to provide a fairly comprehensive list of reported side effects from the shot.

As they reported, New Zealand's health department proudly touted the programme as "the most extensive national immunisation programme against hepatitis B in the world". However, they quickly took a more sober view, once the programme got underway. After only three months, the Hamilton Department of Health faxed to hepatitis B coordinators in all area health boards a message from the principal medical officers, indicating they had received reports of allergic life-threatening shock in children receiving the HB vaccine.

A year later, the medical assessor for adverse events tallied the many side effects suffered by the children, including lethargy and malaise; diarrhoea; asthma; arthritis; Guillain-Barre syndrome, faintness, pallor, loss of consciousness; and drop in blood pressure. The report noted that the incidence of adverse events could have been close to one in every 50 children after their first dose.

As a result of these problems, the NZ health department, its tail between its legs, brought the vaccination programme to an abrupt halt.

Immune-system suppression
In the early 1990s, SmithKline and French was licensed to produce the genetically engineered version of the vaccine, which is grown on yeast cells. In April 1992, a concerned New Zealand physician prepared a report on the use of the

recombinant hepatitis B vaccine in newborns. In it, he says: "I believe giving the hepatitis B vaccine with DPT (diphtheria-pertussis-tetanus triple shot) and/or polio vaccine causes significant immune suppression in a significant number of children, as witnessed by the number of recurrent infections.... These events often happen when previous DPT, DT (diphtheria-tetanus only), or polio vaccines have been well tolerated on their own. . . . When we were giving hepatitis B vaccination at birth, there were a number of children who had prolonged post-natal jaundices, lasting up to two or three weeks. This was not something that I had observed in the preceding 15 years, and, again, I have not seen it since the early immunisation has been stopped."

Hepatitis B and kidney disease

The biggest problem with the new HB vaccine is that there's a good deal we don't know about it. Although the American Centers for Disease Control recommends that all newborn babies get the shot, top medical authorities basically admit that we don't really know whether it is effective, what the side effects are in babies and children, or even when the effect wears off.

The hepatitis B vaccine has been linked with the kidney disease glomerulonephritis. The Lancet (January 23, 1993) reports the case of a 21-year-old man who developed the condition after a third booster of HB vaccine.

Glomerulonephritis causes swelling, increased urination—including the passing of protein—a fall in blood pressure and possibly even renal failure. Other established side effects of HB vaccines are inflammation of the nerves, severe skin eruptions and eye problems.

The 1991 edition of *The Red Book*, produced by the American Academy of Pediatrics, published the report of the

Committee on Infectious Diseases of the AAP, which says that routine screening of mothers-to-be for HB virus is "recommended", not mandatory—tacit acknowledgement that the shot itself is only necessary for the newborns of infected mothers.

Elsewhere in the volume, the AAP admits that the duration of protection and the need for booster doses is "not yet fully divined". And between 30 and 50 per cent of people vaccinated with three doses of the vaccine lose detectable antibodies within seven years. This could mean that you may need a booster shot every five years for the rest of your life. Again, the AAP admits this with the statement that "the possible need for booster doses after longer intervals than five to seven years will be assessed as additional information becomes available".

Finally, the AAP says that in 1–2 per cent of cases "the recommended regimen. . . is not effective. Therefore, infants should be tested at nine months or later to see if it's taken." This means that two out of every 100 babies won't be protected by the vaccine.

An even higher failure rate has been found in adults; a study published in the Journal of Infectious Diseases (1992; 165: 7-8) showed that 10 per cent of volunteers vaccinated failed to produce antibodies. There is also the possibility that the hepatitis B vaccine can itself cause a mutant strain of the virus. In a study in southern Italy published in The Lancet (1990; 336: 325-9), 44 of the 1,590 infants born of HB carriers became HB positive, 32 of whom showed evidence of infection and one showed serious disease. The study group concluded that the vaccine caused a viral "escape" mutation—that is, a slightly different organism resistant to the protective effects of the vaccine. It has been estimated that 3 per cent of babies born to mothers given the hepatitis B vaccine go on to develop a mutated form of hepatitis B (The Lancet, 1990; 336: 325-9).

Another Lancet correspondent noted that failure to detect these mutants may lead to transmission of the HBV through donated blood. In fact, it has been documented that these viral mutants can be transmitted via contaminated blood products, causing severe hepatitis. And of course, this mutant may affect individuals even if they have been vaccinated (The Lancet, 1994; 343: 737-8).

Another study showed that patients vaccinated with HB had a mixture of these mutants and the usual form of hepatitis B virus, as well as mild hepatitis. But those patients whose blood had the mutant on its own eventually suffered the more severe liver disease (Gastroenterology, 1992; 102: 538-43).

Some 12,000 adverse events linked with the hepatitis B vaccine have been reported to the American Vaccine Adverse Events Reporting System between 1990 and 1994. The reports numbered some serious injuries including hospitalisation or death. A large fraction included adults given the hepatitis B vaccine on its own (Ohio Parents for Vaccine Safety, Vaccine News, Summer 1995). Other rare side effects include abdominal cramps, arthagia, Stevens Johnson syndrome, paralysis, Bell's palsy, MS and anaphylactic shock.

One bizarre side effect is hair loss. US doctors investigating reports of hair loss in children after immunisation have found it is a common complaint unacknowledged by the Food and Drug Administration (FDA).

Dr Robert Wise and associates identified 60 cases of hair loss between 1978 and 1995, though the FDA only had nine on file. One mother told the FDA her child's hair fell out on two separate occasions, shortly after injections of the hepatitis B vaccine.

Dr Samuel Sepkowitz from Oklahoma City, Oklahoma,

says since the report was published he has been notified of an average of one case of hair loss due to vaccination per week (JAMA, 1998; 279: 117-8).

J Barthelow Classen, director of American-based Classen Immuno-Therapies in Baltimore, Maryland, has provided some astonishing evidence of the relationship between childhood immunisation and the development of diabetes mellitis.

Classen and his research team evaluated the effect of the recent hepatitis b immunisation programme in New Zealand on the development of insulin-dependent diabetes.

Classen located the Christchurch diabetes registry, the only such registry in New Zealand, which has followed the health of a group of 100,000 people under 20 since 1982 (Care, 1992; 15: 895-9; Care, 1995; 18: 1428-33). Between 1982 to 1987, before the launch of the New Zealand hepatitis B campaign, the registry recorded the incidence of diabetes at 11.2 cases per 100,000 people every year.

From 1989 to 1991, the years immediately following the vaccination campaign, the incidence of diabetes leapt to 18.2 cases per 100,000 per year—an increase of 60 per cent.

"We . . . believe the most likely explanation is that the immunisation programme caused the diabetes epidemic," writes Classen.

The data Classen has collected also indicates that diabetes epidemics have followed the recent widespread use of *haemophilus influenza b* vaccine.

Classen believes that the mechanism by which the damage occurs is no mystery. The manufacturers of the hepatitis B vaccine acknowledged that the vaccine can cause a number of autoimmune diseases.

Other studies have shown that the hepatitis B vaccine, among other vaccines, has the potential of causing insulin-dependent diabetes because it releases interferons. These interferons have been shown to cause autoimmune disease, including insulin dependent diabetes (Science, 1993; 260: 1942-6; Diabetes, 1995; 44: 658-64; Ann Intern Med, 1995; 123: 318).

THE VACCINATION BIBLE

Chapter ten

C H I C K E N P O X

After the US Food and Drug Administration approved the licence of the chickenpox vaccine Varivax, by then supplier Merck, Sharp & Dohme, in November 1995 the American Academy of Pediatrics announced that it should be given to all American children between the ages of one and 18 who haven't had chickenpox.

The FDA recommends a single injection for children between 12 months and 12 years and two shots, four to eight weeks apart, for teenagers and adults. Although Merck has been reported to be considering a licence in Britain, so far the drug company hasn't applied. One possible reason is that its vaccine is currently only made in frozen form, and freezers aren't generally available in the surgeries of British GPs. Japan and Korea have also licensed similar products using the same strain (Oka) of the live, attenuated virus, and several other countries have licensed it for children at risk (those with lowered immunity).

The arguments behind the approval of the chickenpox vaccine carry an air of desperation—a vaccine searching for a rationale. There's no doubt that chickenpox in a healthy child is only a minor nuisance. Four million cases occur in the US, according to the US Centers for Disease Control and Prevention (CDC)—usually among children under 15. Most reported cases of chickenpox in children under 10 are mild and death is rare. However, the CDC points out that some

9,000 people with chickenpox are hospitalised, and 50 to 100 of those catching the disease—mostly young children with lowered immunity—die.

The main population at risk of complications are children with leukaemia who are having chemotherapy, which depresses the immune system, or children and adults taking drugs like steroids for asthma or other illnesses with a similar kind of effect on the immune system.

Besides the immunocompromised, babies and adults can suffer from more severe side effects, such as pneumonia, bacterial superinfection, encephalitis, arthritis, hepatitis and glomerulonephritis (an inflammation of the kidneys). If pregnant women contract the virus in the first two trimesters of pregnancy, it can cause birth defects of the skin, limbs, eyes and nervous system; in the last trimester of pregnancy, the baby can contract chickenpox, which has up to a 30 per cent mortality in this age group (BMJ, January 7, 1995).

Most young children who contract chickenpox don't suffer very badly with it, and so there is little point in their being vaccinated against such a mild condition. Only those whose immunity is lowered in some way stand to gain any potential benefit. This means that all parents are being asked to expose their healthy children to the risk of the vaccine's side-effects purely for the benefit of this small-risk population. Furthermore, since no one knows how long the vaccine's effects will last, healthy vaccinated children may be at risk of developing the disease as adults when it is often more serious.

An economic decision

The main reason for launching the jab appears to be economic. Several researchers have attempted to quantify the financial cost of cases of chickenpox. In fact, the cost of treating chickenpox is very low—mainly because there isn't much you can do other than sit it out—far lower than the cost of each jab, at $39. (The entire vaccine programme costs $162m a year in the US.) However, to make the cost-benefit equation lean heavily towards immunisation, the authorities have thrown in the amount of parental income or work time lost when a child has to stay home with chickenpox. This is calculated as $293 per family, or $183 per chickenpox cases (Ped Infec Dis J, 1994; 13: 173-7). (The days lost are often more than the child actually needs because many schools have policies forcing children to stay at home well past the stage when the disease is contagious.) Therefore, the net theoretical benefit of this vaccination is a saving of some $6.6m of lost income in the US alone (J Ped, June 1994).

Other journals have somehow increased this into a $400m savings (Lancet, 16 April 1994). Of course, this highly theoretical figure doesn't take into account the many thousands of parents who will be able to claim paid leave. It also doesn't take into account the total cost of vaccinating adolescents ($329 per chickenpox case prevented), which actually doesn't make economic sense (Ped, May 1995).

A benign disease

Many questions remain about the effect of vaccinating a population against a disease that doesn't do much harm. The CDC has admitted that considerable uncertainty exists about a wholesale vaccination of pre-schoolers (JAMA, 22-29 June 1994.)

Why aren't we simply vaccinating children at risk (or, better yet, looking for alternate ways of treating diseases like leukaemia that don't involve suppressing the immune system)? But ironically, the Merck vaccine is not supposed to be used in the very population it is meant to protect—those on immunosuppressive drugs. Merck warns that vaccination with the live chickenpox virus can result in a more extensive

123

vaccine-associated rash or disseminated disease in individuals on immunosuppressant doses of corticosteroids.

Even for children with leukaemia, who are on an experimental protocol, the vaccine hasn't proved wholly effective; 5–10 per cent have developed a mild infection during vaccination and about 10 per cent had breakthrough chickenpox within three years (Public Citizens Health Letter, August 1995). In one study, 40-50 per cent of children with leukaemia developed a vaccine-associated rash, although the study said 90 per cent were protected (Rev Infec Dis, Nov-Dec 1991). In another study, this protection lasted eight to 10 years (J Infec Dis, August 1992).

No one, not even the manufacturers, knows how long the vaccine works for. In its handout on the drug, Merck admits the duration of protection from varicella infection after vaccination with Varivax is unknown.

Although those in favour of the vaccine argue that children show evidence of antibodies for at least six years (J Infec Dis, January 1994), and that booster shots can always be given, the vaccine doesn't work as well among adults, conferring only 70 per cent protection (Rev Infec Disease, 1991; 13 Suppl 11: S957-9).

However, all that any scientific study can do is to measure antibody levels, which may not be a true picture of whether someone is adequately protected. In one study of 14 healthy children who'd contracted chickenpox naturally, three lost any evidence of antibodies or immunity (Ped Infec Dis J, 1991; 10: 569-75). In another study of 21 pregnant women, four developed the disease even though they'd had prior evidence of antibodies from naturally occurring chickenpox. The study concluded that the criteria for determining immunity from the chickenpox zoster virus remains ill-defined (J Infec Dis, 1994; 170: 991-5).

We also have no idea at what point children require boosters so that a repeat of the US situation with measles doesn't recur. In the late 1980s and early 1990s, epidemics of measles occurred among college-age teenagers and young adults, most of whom had been vaccinated against measles as children because the vaccine wore off once they reached maturity.

Furthermore, its thought that even immunised patients require re-exposure to natural chickenpox or re-immunisation in order to boost long-term immunity. Although it is planned that this vaccine will be given with the measles-mumps-rubella triple jab, it has been shown not to work as well when given at the same time as the Hib vaccine.

Not-so-minor side-effects

Merck says that about a fifth of all recipients have swelling, rash or the like at the injection site, 15 per cent have a fever of 30°C or higher, and about 7 per cent have a chickenpox rash at the injection site or locally. Otherwise, 21 per cent of patients reported an adverse reaction, including (in decreasing order of frequency): upper respiratory illness, cough, irritability/nervousness, fatigue, disturbed sleep, diarrhoea, loss of appetite, vomiting, ear infection, nappy or contact rash, headache, teething, malaise, abdominal pain, nausea, eye complaints, chills, enlargement of the lymph nodes, myalgia, lower respiratory illness, allergic reactions (including allergic rash and hives), stiff neck, heat rash, prickly heat, arthralgia, eczema, dry skin or dermatitis, constipation and itching. Adults have reported similar side effects, albeit with far less frequency.

However, what doctors don't tell you is that around one in every 100 children vaccinated with Varivax have gone on to develop pneumonia, and one in a thousand have febrile seizures. In one study of 3,303 children, one 16-month-old baby was hospitalised with rash, fever and swelling of the right knee 16 days after the vaccine (Ped, May 1991), and one adult developed a severe kidney inflammation after the jab (Clin Infec Dis, 1993; 17: 1079).

Furthermore, these reactions, including fever and rash, can happen at any point for six weeks after vaccination and last for six days or more—refuting the notion that parents are going to save time off work by vaccination (Ped, Sept 1991).

It may make sense for children and adults at risk to consider the vaccine, although acyclovir and varicella immunoglobulin have demonstrated some effectiveness in preventing the illness in at-risk children exposed to the virus. Otherwise, healthy children, who are already pin cushions for nine diseases, may be trading a mild childhood illness for a load of adult problems without much appreciable gain.

Chickenpox and waning immunity

The problem with waning immunity is that the chickenpox vaccine may create a population of adults at greater risk of serious illness than they would have been if they'd got chickenpox as children. It could turn what is largely a benign childhood disease into a source of major illness and hospitalisation. Indeed, in one study of the vaccine, the number of cases of chickenpox in adults did increase (cited in JAMA, 22/29 June 1994).

Another concern is the effect of injecting into one-year-old babies and children a live virus which has a tendency to lie latent in the nervous system and reactivate many years later. A majority of patients who have had chickenpox as children may go on to develop herpes zoster, commonly known as shingles, later in life. This condition causes painful and highly sensitive blisters on the skin along the nerves infected by the virus, often on only one side of the body. The severe pain may last from two to five weeks and in older patients, this jabbing pain can go on for several months.

There is some evidence that the live chickenpox vaccine can incubate in the body, causing shingles in later life. At least three cases of shingles have been reported in healthy children given the vaccine (J Infec Dis, May 1989), and one in a healthy adult (J Infect Dis, September 1989). This, of course, means that the vaccine cannot accomplish its stated aim—to wipe out the zoster virus altogether. In one small study, 11 children developing a rash after vaccine were found to have the shingles virus (Ped, May 1991).

We also don't know whether the live vaccine virus is itself contagious. According to Merck's information sheet, individuals vaccinated with Varivax may potentially be capable of transmitting the vaccine virus to close contacts.

Perhaps the greatest worry is the likelihood that future babies will be more susceptible to chickenpox once this generation of vaccinated girls is unable to pass on maternal immunity. With measles in 1990, the largest increases in the incidence rates of the disease occurred among babies under one (137 per cent) and adults over 25 (130 per cent) (JAMA, 26 June 1991).

Although many studies demonstrate a very high take-up rate among children—70–90 per cent or more demonstrate antibodies to the disease—there is also a high incidence of what has been termed breakthrough cases—that is, vaccinated children who have gone on to develop chickenpox. In one study, one-fifth of vaccinated children went on to develop chickenpox, although it was a more mild form of the illness.

In another study, conducted by Merck itself, 12 per cent of 3,303 vaccinated children caught chickenpox when exposed to it at home (Ped, May 1991). As for adults, 27 per cent of a Merck-studied group which received two doses of Varivax developed chickenpox when exposed to it in the household over two years (**WDDTY**, 1996; 6 (12): 8, 10-11).

Chapter eleven

MENINGITIS C

On November 1 of last year, Liam Donaldson, the Department of Health's chief medical officer, announced the launching of a mass vaccination campaign against the group C strain of meningococcal meningitis. "By the end of next year," Donaldson confidently announced, "we hope to have confined this particular strain of meningitis largely to the history books."

Unusually for vaccine programmes in this country, which ordinarily copycats products and vaccine programmes formulated in other countries—chiefly America—this vaccine is true, blue British. Not only is the vaccine born and bred in Britain, but this is the only country to have launched a mass vaccination campaign against meningitis to date.

So confident were the powers that be about initial studies of the new, improved vaccine that they pushed forward the intended launch date by a year. At a time when the National Health Service was more strapped than ever for cash, Donaldson and Dr David Salisbury, the DoH's principle medical officer, managed to garner £10 million to launch an ambitious scheme which would innoculate all of the nation's 14 million school children within a year.

The plan was to vaccinate the entire pool of children in stages, beginning with those most at risk—teenagers aged 15 to 17, then babies under a year, who would receive the jab at the same time they were given the standard first collection of shots. Last month, supplies permitting, the government was to move on to children aged one to five, who would receive it with their MMR booster jabs. As yet more supplies became available, the rest of the population of children would be offered the jab, with the plan to reach the bulk of Britain's children by the summer.

Although the new vaccine wasn't to be ready until November, the government paved the way for publicity about it in August by launching a vaccine drive for university students, who would receive the old A and C combined polysaccharide vaccine. Although the old vaccine is considered less effective and shorter lasting than the new one, the idea, said a DoH spokesperson, was that at least the vaccine would see the nation's 480,000 freshmen students through their three-year university tenure.

But behind the smiles at the DoH and all the self-congratulatory back patting lies a rash decision and all the makings of a scandal not dissimilar to that of the measles campaign of 1994. At that time, all the nation's school children were pressed into receiving a booster measles jab, supposedly to ward off a predicted measles epidemic. The epidemic never arrived, but at least several hundred families are currently suing vaccine manufacturers over apparent brain damage, paralysis and even death suffered by their children allegedly due to the measles booster.

With the new meningitis vaccine, the press has whipped up a fury over the limited supplies of the old vaccine, which were inadequate to meet the demands of the university students. In focusing on the shortage, journalists have missed the real scandal here, which has to do with expediency and, inevitably, politics. In the wholly laudable desire to staunch the increasing number of meningitis cases on the part of all involved, an alliance with no checks and balances has been forged between a government wishing to be regarded as heroic and a private company, with its need to turn a profit. In the process, our entire population of children are being exploited as a giant, convenient pool of guinea pigs.

Not an epidemic

Much has been made of meningitis as a random killer of children, and there is no doubt that it is horrendous and frightening in its rapid, potentially fatal onset. But just how much actual risk does your child face?

Although the plan is to give all children the vaccine, rather than simply individual groups at high risk, children between five and fifteen are at virtually no risk of contracting meningitis C. In the five-year period between 1994 and 1999, group C meningococcal disease killed approximately 20 babies under one, 21 babies aged one, 18 two year olds, approximately 15 three year olds, a handful of four, five and six year olds, and almost no other children under adolescence.

After babies are a year old, they develop active immunity by being exposed to a non-pathogenic form of meningococcus.

Casualties did not pick up again until the age of fifteen through twenty, the so-called highest cluster. In this age category, meningitis killed some 12 fifteen year olds, approximately 30 sixteen year olds, 12 seventeen year olds, about 18 eighteen year olds, about 18 nineteen year olds, and 10 twenty year olds over five years. So, in total, the disease killed approximately 200 young children, or an average of 40 children a year (70 a year in 1999).

While no one wishes to denigrate the tragic loss of these lives, in strictly epidemiological terms, the death rate of this form of meningitis is small potatoes.

It rates well behind many accidents as conditions which account for appreciable numbers of childhood deaths. For instance, your baby is five times more likely to drown in his bathtub and 86 times more likely to die of cot death than die from meningitis C. Six times as many children and young adults get

131

knocked over and killed by cars than die of meningitis C. British traffic deaths of all varieties among children—representing the highest fatalities among this age group in all of Europe—claim the lives of 1,309 children and young adults every year—more than 32 times the rate of meningitis deaths.

If there were an average of 50 childhood deaths from meningitis C in 1998 and there are 14 million British children, generally speaking, your child's chances of catching this disease at the moment are one in 200,000, with slightly higher risks in babyhood and late teens. However, it is the tragic swiftness of the disease's deadly progress and the existence of so-called local clusters that placed the disease on the front pages. Media coverage, more than the actual prevalence of the disease, accounts for its high profile and also for the irrational fear instilled in the public mind about it.

No one would wish to put a price tag on the heads of these dead children. But one must question the wisdom of throwing such heavy economic resources at a disease with such relatively small fatalities, rather than simply concentrating on groups at high risk: those without spleens, with chronic underlying illness, and in crowded or impoverished conditions.

Heikki Peltola, professor of infectious diseases and pediatrician at the University of Helsinki and the Hospital for Children and Adolescents, confirmed that although the UK has a higher per capita incidence of this disease than other countries do, including his native Finland, "The question was whether the incidence of this diease was high enough to merit mass immunisation. In no country is there an epidemic of this disease." As he wrote recently in an article about meningitis vaccination (Drugs, 1998; 55: 347-66): "Generally speaking, the incidence of meningococcal disease is too low to indicate vaccinations for the whole population, or even children, but some risk groups and epidemics are important exceptions."

A deadlier form of meningitis

The British government has touted *Neisseria meningitidis* group C as the most deadly bacterium causing meningococcal disease, which affected 1,530 people in Britain last year and claims the lives of one-tenth of those who contract it.

But not according to the DoH's own "factsheet". Group C meningococcal disease, which began appearing only a decade ago, accounts for only 40 per cent of cases of meningitis contracted in Britain and elsewhere. Between 1994-9, meningitis B killed nearly 70 infants under one. This incidence represents more than three times the number of deaths of meningitis C among this age group during the same period. Strain B also killed twice as many one year olds as did strain C. In all, meningitis B killed approximately 170 children under six—which represents the same number of deaths from meningitis C among all age groups combined. Although meningitis C is the major cause of meningococcal death among teenagers, accounting for 80 per cent of deaths (meningitis B only claimed the lives of about 24 teenagers and young adults), the B version is far more deadly to babies and small children, representing at least two-thirds of all meningococcal deaths in this age group.

David Hall, corporate affairs manager for Wyeth, who developed the new vaccine, says that so far, producing a vaccine for the B strain has proved elusive. "B has structural differences, having to do with one of antigens on the polysaccharide protein code," he says. "For some reason, that makes it difficult to come up with a workable vaccine."

Dr Richard Nicholson, editor of the Bulletin of Medical Ethics, is concerned that even if this vaccine proves 100 per cent effective, it will protect against only a minority of meningococcal cases. Nevertheless, its existence could cause the public to become complacent about watching for warning signs of the disease caused by the other strains.

A "new, improved" version?

The old combined A and C meningitis vaccine was a "polysaccharide", made of a bit of the coat that forms the bacterial wall of *Neisseria meningitidis* strain C. Like the old Hib meningitis polysaccharide vaccine, it doesn't work very well. So Wyeth created a "conjugated" version, which would marry the polysaccharide of the strain C bug with CRM_{197}, a diphtheria toxin, which has, as far as the vaccine community sees it, a proven track record in stimulating the immune system and getting it to work.

By piggybacking C strain cells onto a proven entity, the idea, says Wyeth's David Hall, is that the CRM cells put the body on red alert that it is under attack. Under this heightened situation, it is more likely then to recognise the polysaccharide cells as foreign and worthy of developing antibodies and memory cells, which help the body remember how to generate specific antibodies in the future if needed.

At least that's the theory. Nevertheless, numerous studies show substantial vaccine failure rates among the supposedly successful Hib conjugate vaccine. One study showed the protective effect of one conjugate Hib vaccine was only 74 per cent (Lancet, 1991; 338: 395-8), and only 35 per cent among Alaskan infants, who are at higher risk of Hib meningitis than other children.

Another study showed that 52 per cent of Hib meningitis cases occurred among vaccinated children (Pediatrics, 1995; 96: 424-7).

And has the Hib vaccine eliminated Hib meningitis? It's true there's been a drastic drop in cases. But that's consistent with previously identified cyclic variation in this disease, with certain peaks and troughs in its incidence (JAMA, 1993; 269: 227-31).

Furthermore, the incidence has also fallen among babies who

haven't been vaccinated (Lancet, 1997; 349: 1197-1201). The supposed Hib vaccine success story could be nothing more than the cyclical downturn in a disease. It's too early to tell.

Immunity for life?

This vaccine will offer teenagers "almost 100 per cent immunity for life", wrote the Times, and the DoH confirms that besides babies, who will get three doses, a single dose is sufficient in all other children. In the very first edition of **What Doctors Don't Tell You**, we quoted then health minister Edwina Currie claiming that the new triple measles-mumps-rubella (MMR) vaccine would offer "life-long protection with a single jab". Five years later, the British government launched the countrywide booster campaign, after massive epidemics of measles among previously vaccinated youngsters in America proved that the MMR does not, after all, give you protection for life.

If the meningitis vaccine works similarly—and most vaccines appear to wane over a decade—then teenagers and young adults vaccinated as babies and toddlers will experience waning immunity just at a point where they are most vulnerable to the disease.

Besides not knowing how long this vaccine will last, no one is sure how many shots and of which variety will confer long-term protection.

In one study of 114 infants from West Gloucestershire, babies were randomly divided into groups receiving either a 2 mcg or 10 mcg dose of meningococcal C vaccine. Then, half the infants received the old A and C polysaccharide vaccine at 15-20 months. (The others were to receive this booster at age 4.)

Among those getting the lower initial dose, bactericidal antibody titres rose at five months but fell by 14 months to not much higher than they were originally (1: 4 to 1:1057 to 1: 19). With those receiving the 10 mcg dose, antibody responses were significantly higher at five months than in the 2 mcg group, but were lower after boosting with the plain polysaccharide vaccine than with the lower dose group.

This appears to mean that 1) the government believes that boosters will be necessary at some point and is probably already planning for them and 2) nobody really knows which combination of vaccines—higher or lower doses for initial shot and follow-up boosters—is really going to work, or whether using the old polysaccharide vaccine actually lowers your immunity, as it appears to in one study (J Infect Dis, 1999; 179: 1569-72).

The researchers say in the conclusion of their report that "total antibody levels required for protection against serogroup C disease are *not known* (italics ours).

In another study, also by the PHLS (J Infect Dis, 1996; 174; 1360-3) of a conjugate meningococcal combination A and C product, antibodies also fell rapidly 12 to 14 months later, even after three doses.

Because the antibody levels fell so rapidly, the PHLS addressed itself to what it says is the good news—the presence of immunologic "memory". The Hib vaccination, they claim, offers long-term protection despite the fact that antibody levels fall rapidly with that vaccine as well. As the Hib vaccine has only been around for a handful of years, time will tell whether that theory is correct.

According to Wyeth's David Hall, the old "polysaccharide" vaccine works at best 75 per cent of the time on older children and wears off after a few years. It does not work in babies and toddlers. The new "conjugated" variety, called Meningitec, has produced immunological "memory" cells in babies and toddlers by being piggybacked onto the diphtheria toxoid, which is mainly responsible for the red-alert immune-system response. The existence of these memory cells, he says, means that it's likely the vaccine will last longer, but nobody knows for sure. "We know that this is a sign of long-lasting immunity," says Hall, "but until you embark on a mass vaccination programme, you're never going to prove it."

Lucky for Wyeth, then, to be located in Britain. Several years ago, the DoH and its government sidekick, the Public Health Laboratory Service, which studies, monitors and formulates immunisation policy, approached Wyeth and other vaccine companies, asking them to step up research into a meningitis C vaccine and even offering to help research it.

When Wyeth got to the finish line first with a product, the PHLS basically took over its testing. Many of the larger trials were conducted by the PHLS.

"One way we were able to bring forward our launch date was because we worked together in collaboration with the DoH," says Hall. Rather than our company having to set up trials, the PHLS did much of the studies for us."

In other words, Wyeth was able to fasttrack this drug through the usual drug-approval procedure, which ordinarily requires a drug company to set up its own trials. The government is then supposed to act as an independent judge, approving them on the basis of safety and effectiveness. In this instance, defendant, prosecution, judge and jury were all effectively on the same team.

A further wrinkle on might be labelled a conflict of interest has to do with the monitoring system of the Public Health Laboratory Service. In 1994, the PHLS devised a surveillance system for monitoring side effects of vaccines. This was first tested out with the all-country measles booster scheme, leading the cynical to wonder whether the mass measles campaign was manufactured in order to test out the effectiveness of the new system.

By working with the PHLS, the third party in the collaboration, Wyeth ensured not only that its studies had the most positive spin possible, but also that the product would be given a blessing to be test-marketed on a mass basis through this new surveillance system. As Hall says, no one would know the effectiveness of the vaccine until it was mass marketed. In effect, the government is carrying out the best post-market testing that Wyeth could ever have dreamt of.

Illness from the jab

The vaccine is highly safe, says the DoH, or "harmless", as Heikki Peltola put it. That is an assertion that no one can make about any vaccine, let along a brand new one that is neither tried nor tested. Although the meningitis C vaccine was tested on 6000 British children, and more than 21,000 people outside the UK, these were short-term tests, lasting at most a few weeks, and many of the trials remain unpublished—that is, unavailable to anyone outside of Wyeth or the government.

In the largest of the three published trials shown to **WDDTY**, all conducted partly or entirely by the Public Health Laboratory Service among 114 infants vaccinated at two, three or four months, side effects were only recorded for seven days by parents and a health nurse (J Infect Dis, 1999; 179: 1569-72). Any symptoms outside this window of time probably would not have been associated with the vaccine. Nevertheless, within the small cohort of babies, 26 of those receiving the lower dose and 53 of those receiving the higher dose had systemic symptoms within the first 24 hours from one of three shots.

Although "systemic symptoms" were not defined, they presumably mean that the children were generally ill after the jab. According to this report, more than one-fifth of the jabs—79 out of a total of 344 jabs—made babies in the vaccine groups ill. Seven of the low-dose group and eight of the high-dose group— more than 13 per cent—developed a fever higher than 38 degrees C. Five of the babies had persistent crying for more than one hour in the first day after the vaccine. Nine babies had erythema (reddening of the skin) of more than 2.5 cm and eight had swelling of more than 2.5 cm.

These latter side effects—which consisted of mainly swelling at the injection site—were noted to be less than those caused by the Hib vaccine, leading to the often quoted remark that this vaccine produces fewer reactions than other ones.

In its data sheet, Wyeth reports that systemic reactions usually include crying, irritability, drowsiness, impaired sleeping, anorexia, diarrhoea and vomiting, all conditions that are "common" after vaccination. Nevertheless, the company points out, "there was no evidence that these were related to Meningitec, rather than concomitant vaccines, particularly DTP vaccines"— as most of these have been given at the same time.

Those reactions the company admits "may possibly be related to the vaccine" include headache and myalgia in adults and irritability and drowsiness in younger children.

One baby was hospitalised for a viral illness following the second vaccination, although the PHLS maintains that this illness was not attributable to the vaccine. One baby given the old A and C polysaccharide jab developed a generalized rash, "mild" facial swelling, cough and coryzal (acute rhinitis) symptoms within five hours after vaccination, although these symptoms resolved within two days after oral antihistamines were given. This baby had no evidence of antibodies to A or C meningococcus—in other words, the vaccine didn't work on him. The researchers again concluded that these adverse events, despite happening within hours of the jab, were "not vaccine related".

In one independent case study, a 25-year-old woman developed acute disseminated post vaccinal encephalomyelitis (ADEM) after being vaccinated with the old combination group A and C polysaccharide vaccine (Arq Neuropsiquiatr, 1997; 55: 632-5). The symptoms only disappeared and the lesions on the myelin sheath of her nervous system finally resolved after treatment with high doses of intravenous steroids. As the researchers noted, although most cases of ADEM have been related to other vaccinations or conditions, this case report indicates that it may also be related to exposure to A and C polysaccharide-protein vaccines and meningococcal vaccine. Whether ADEM becomes a new condition in children once the meningitis C vaccine is widely disseminated is anyone's guess.

In an adult study of another meningitic C vaccine which had been conjugated with the tetanus toxoid, half the 30 subjects reported tenderness at the injection site and half erythema, 13 or nearly half reported pain, two reported headache, and one myalgia.

One patient had a fever higher than 38 degrees C five to seven days after vaccination, but this again was discounted because the researchers said it was associated with a viral illness" (Vaccine; 1999; 18: 641-6).

As David Hall says, we won't really know the long-term effects until the product is out in the mass market. Indeed, we won't be sure of anything until virtually every child in Britain has been given the jab.

"There is no evidence that multiple vaccines overload a child's immune system," says the DoH factsheet. But we don't know the effect of this vaccine on other vaccines given at the same time, as this wasn't really tested for, since multiple vaccines are always presumed to be safe before proven dangerous.

Including the meningitis C vaccine on the standard schedule of infant vaccinations now increases to six the number of vaccines given simultaneously to infants at two months of age.

In the British infant study, the researchers admitted that "increased amounts of carrier protein may interfere with immunologic priming with other conjugate vaccines. This should not affect protection induced by this vaccine but may be important in combination conjugate vaccines using the same carrier proteins." This means that the new vaccine may interfere with other conjugate vaccines like the Hib vaccine—although, again, we won't know until we suck it and see.

Squeezing a balloon

Many in the scientific community wonder whether this vaccine will increase other forms of meningitis. A a great deal of evidence shows that vaccines do cause viral or bacterial populations to shift. The introduction of mass polio vaccination has altered the balance in favour of non-polio gut viruses (BMJ, 1961: 1061); in many countries, other types of related paralytic disease have risen as cases of polio have fallen. For instance, since the introduction of the oral polio vaccine (OPV) in China in 1971, the incidence of GBS has increased tenfold.

As Chinese researchers from the Second Hospital of Hebei Medical College wrote, "The widespread use of OPV may have led to [mutation of the virus], resulting in an alteration of the disease and/or to a change in the main epidemic of a type of polio virus (Lancet, 1994; 344: 1026).

All reports show that the incidence of meningitis has roughly doubled in the last few years. Professor Peltola doubts that this vaccination would change the bacterial population as the group C meningitis isn't epidemic.

Nevertheless, there is evidence that the introduction of mass Hib vaccination for a meningitis which was also not an epidemic has caused a higher proliferation of pneumococcal meningitis, the other bacterial form of the disease. The Pediatric Infectious Disease Journal (1992; 18: 6) has made a connection between penicillin resistant strains of pneumococcal meningitis and universal Hib vaccination. Certainly, cases of bacterial meningitis have risen sharply since the Hib vaccine.

With meningitis C, new evidence shows that one strain easily switches to another type very rapidly. Researchers believe that wiping out one strain of bacteria might cause the other strains to flourish (N Engl J Med, 2000; 342: 219-20).

"Trying to eliminate microorganisms and diseases is comparable to squeezing a balloon," said naturopath Harald Gaier. "You push in one side and it only makes the other side bulge."

Mass vaccination blunders

This is not the first time the government has rushed through a vaccination programme in response to a threatened epidemic. In 1976, the American government, warned by scientists that an epidemic of the swine flu was imminent, pressed all American adults to line up for a hastily developed jab. One of every 100,000 Americans given the shot developed Guillain-Barre paralysis from a vaccine that was insufficiently tested for a disease that, in the end, never arrived. The government ended up paying out $93 million in compensation to victims.

More recently, in 1998, the US confidently included a new vaccine for rotavirus, the disease which causes serious dehydrating diarrhoea in babies, among the schedule of vaccines given to 2-month-old infants. Just a year later, Wyeth Lederle Vaccines was forced to withdraw from the market its new vaccine RotaShield, when the Centers for Disease Control and Prevention discovered a link between the vaccine and the development of bowel intussusception, or bowel collapse, in more than 100 infants. Of 102 cases, 29 babies required surgery and seven had bowel resections. One infant died. This for a disease that kills, at most, 20 American babies a year.

No doubt the British government was motivated by nothing but good intentions in rushing through this new meningitis vaccine. But the history of vaccination shows that it is always wise to err on the side of caution. In the US, a vaccine for pneumococcal meningitis under development, also produced by Wyeth, was carefully tested for four years on a sample population of 38,000 children in northern California before being released to the public at large.

In the UK, however, as with the measles epidemic, the DoH is rashly attempting wholesale herd immunity with an untested product, rather than carefully weighing up the risks and benefits of a new, potentially dangerous jab on individual children. One day the government may learn to lead with its head as well as its heart.

If you decide against vaccination with the meningitis C jab. . .

● Impress upon your children the importance of a whole-food diet. Don't keep processed food or soft drinks in the house, so that they eat them only as treats.

● Give them supplements and immune boosters like vitamin A.

● Use echinacea, garlic and other anti-infectives like goldenseal and tea tree oil for the winter months.

● Only have antibiotics administered when absolutely needed, and never for viral infections.

● Teach your children to cook good, healthy food when they are young, so they will know how to feed themselves properly when they leave home.

● Make sure they are living in hygienic and not overly crowded accommodation. If not, help them move.

● During their first year away from home, do whatever you can to make sure they are eating well. Dormitory food is notorious for being unnutritious. Supplement their food with periodic "Care" packages which include supplements.

● Consider giving any child at risk a homoeopathic nosode. The single large-scale trial of homoeopathic nosodes concerns one for meningococcal disease. In 1974, more than 18,000 children were given Meningococcinum IICH prior to an epidemic. Not a single incidence of meningitis was recorded among this population, and not one child suffered any side effects (FX Eizayaga, *Treatis on Homoeopathic Medicine*, Buenos Aires: Ediciones Marcel, 1991). Ainsworth's, the homoeopathic pharmacy, has now produced a homoeopathic version of the meningitis C vaccine (020 7 935 5330).

● Stay alert for early signs of meningitis—the pinprick rash, stiff neck, fever, vomiting, severe headache—and rush your child to the doctor at the first sign of anything suspicious. If it is bacterial meningitis, antibiotics can save his life.

Chapter twelve

TRAVEL VACCINES: NO PASSPORT TO SAFETY

Most travellers heading anywhere but Europe or North America resemble human pin cushions by the time their doctor has given them all their shots. The question of travel vaccines is difficult because doctors usually don't admit that 1) they have no idea what you ought to have in various countries and that 2) the medical literature shows that many of these shots won't protect you, anyway.

Government policy for travellers abroad is a case of massive overkill. A handful of vaccines are urged—and sometimes even forced—on you anytime you venture much beyond our shores. If you were to listen to the UK Department of Health's recommendations "Health Advice for Travellers" or the Centers for Disease Control and Prevention in the US, you'd get vaccinated against polio every time you stepped foot outside Europe, North America or Australia, even though the disease is virtually non-existent in many of these recommended areas.

The problem with this "just in case" mindset is not only that it creates a paranoiac view of the world, but also that it offers travellers a false assurance that a simple jab can take the place of careful precaution when heading off to remote areas. Furthermore, it rests on the assumption that these jabs actually work. Of all the vaccines, travel vaccines have the poorest record of success. The old cholera vaccine has such a dismal track record that it may be one reason the World Health Organisation (WHO) has dropped it from the list of required immunisations and no country requires it anymore.

With malaria there is not only no vaccine, but a dangerous and growing resistance to the drugs used to treat it.

With travel vaccines, more than any other, it's vital to find out how necessary, how safe and how effective each one is before you make your travel plans, particularly to less well trod areas.

RISK AREAS

Cholera
Cholera is a growing problem in areas in South America, Middle East, Africa and Asia where sanitation is poor. Vaccination is only recommended if you are travelling to cholera areas across remote borders, especially overland.

Hepatitis A
Little risk of infection in industrialised countries. Infection risk increases where sanitation is primitive.

Hepatitis B
Developed areas, such as the US, western Europe and Australia, are relatively low risk. Significantly greater risk occurs in developing countries, such as China, South-East Asia, Africa, the Pacific islands, Haiti, the Dominican Republic, parts of the Middle East and the Amazon Basin.

Japanese encephalitis
There are three main risk areas: the Far East, the Indian subcontinent, South-East Asia.

Malaria
Travellers to Africa are at risk. In Asia and South America,

there is little risk of exposure in towns or resorts or if you are travelling to rural areas in daylight hours.

Measles
All developing countries suffer, especially in poor, overcrowded areas, with a seasonal increase in winter and spring. Frequent epidemics ravage the sub-Saharan belt across the middle of Africa (especially during the December–June dry season). Occasional epidemics hit Burundi, Kenya, Tanzania, northern India and Nepal.

Polio
There have been no recent cases in the west, but thousands are reported each year in developing countries in Africa, Asia, the Middle East and Eastern Europe. The British Department of Health recommends everyone travelling outside north and western Europe, North America and Australasia should be protected.

Rabies
Dog rabies is common in parts of Mexico, Colombia, Ecuador, El Salvador, Guatemala, India, Nepal, Peru, the Philippines, Sri Lanka, Thailand and Vietnam. It also occurs in most other countries in Africa, Asia, and South and Central America. Vaccination before travel is only necessary for those exposed to an unusual risk of infection, such as taking long journeys in the bush.

Typhoid
Travellers to industrialised countries are at little risk. Warm countries with primitive sanitation pose the greatest risk, especially developing countries in Latin America, Asia and Africa.

Yellow Fever
Occurs in tropical areas of Africa and South America.

Meningitis
Meningococcal meningitis is prevalent in some areas of Africa and Asia. Saudi Arabia requires immunisation of all those going on the Hajj, the great annual Muslim pilgrimage.

Malaria
Of all infectious diseases abroad, malaria is perhaps your greatest risk. WHO estimates that there are 300–500m people infected with malaria, the parasitic disease carried by the Anopheles mosquito (JAMA, 1996; 275: 230-233). Each year in Britain, 2,000 people contract malaria and 12 people die, a higher figure than from any other tropical disease. (In America, where presumably fewer people travel to Asia and Africa, several hundred patients contract it every year).

There is no reliable vaccine for malaria, so the rationale has been that taking the drugs which treat malaria as prophylactics (just-in-case measure) before, during and after your stay in the infected area will also somehow ward off the disease.

Several synthetic anti-malaria drugs, developed during World War II, are no longer effective. The problem is that most strains of the disease have developed active resistance to the drugs. Few tropical countries are now unaffected by strains resistant to chloroquine, often used with proguanil (Paludrine), the former drugs of choice; resistance to quinine, an earlier favourite, is also now increasing.

Consequently, doctors and even tropical vaccine experts are finding it difficult to tell patients which types of drugs work where anymore. They tend to rely on a quick-change scheme of swapping schedules of drugs frequently in the hope of outwitting resistant strains. The same applies to patients who return with malaria; the choice of treatment depends on the parasite's resistance to the drug in the area where you got the infection (New Eng J Med, 1996; 335: 800-6).

The general rule of thumb at the moment is to use combinations of drugs in areas where resistance is known not to be high (BMJ, 1993; 307: 1041; New Eng J of Med, 1996; 335: 800-6). There is also the fragile balance which must be maintained between the risk of the disease and the risk of the drugs. There are a number of toxic effects with all these drugs, such as nausea, vomiting, severe gastrointestinal disturbances and even psychotic reactions.

Chloroquine can cause bone marrow suppression, heart problems, a neuropsychiatric syndrome and brain dysfunction. *The British Compendium of Data Sheets 1996-7* also lists skin eruptions, itching, hair loss and skin de-pigmentation. Prolonged high doses of chloroquine can lead to damage to the retina of the eyes, ringing of the ears or convulsions. One doctor reported that his six-year-old son had a grand mal seizure after taking the drug (BMJ, 1996; 312: 1421).

Other sulphur drugs such as sulphadoxine-purimethamine are effective but also cause rapid development of resistant strains (Lancet, 1996; 347: 244-8). The natural compound quinine, made from cinchona bark, remains more than 85 per cent effective nearly everywhere and has been a mainstay of malaria treatment for three centuries. Nevertheless, it is starting to lose its effectiveness in South-East Asia. It also can be toxic, causing dysphoria, tinnitus and high-tone deafness, hypoglycaemia and even serious cardiovascular or nervous-system effects (New Eng J Med, 1996; 335: 69-75 and 800-6).

As drug resistance grew, so tropical disease experts turned to mefloquine, marketed as Lariam by Swiss pharmaceutical giant Hoffman-La Roche. Besides its effectiveness, this once-a-week anti-malarial quickly became popular because of its convenience (Lancet, 1996; 348: 344). However, because it tends to stay in the system for a long time, the potential for adverse reactions also appears heightened. Side effects include severe psychological disturbances, such as panic attacks and hallucinations, vomiting, dizziness, headache, hair loss, seizures, tinnitus, emotional problems and at least one instance of heart attack (*Compendium of Data Sheets, 1996-7*). Mefloquine also causes far more adverse neuropsychiatric episodes than proguanil or chloroquine (BMJ, 1996; 313: 525-8). In addition, 500 British travellers who claim to be suffering from severe and long-term effects of mefloquine are taking the company to court for compensation (Guardian, 30 August 1996). The death of a six-year-old girl who was taking the drug has increased calls for greater controls (Guardian and The Times, 27 January 1997). And now holfantrine is being looked at as a possible new drug, although there is evidence of toxicity to the heart (Lancet, 1993; 341: 1044-49).

Hopes had been pinned on trials of SPf66, a new vaccine developed by a team in Colombia. After a series of studies, protection was found to be only 31 per cent, but was nevertheless considered encouraging (Lancet, 1994; 344: 1172-3). However, a later randomised, double-blind trial study of infants in the Gambia showed that the vaccine was useless, as did a study of children in northwestern Thailand (Lancet, 1995; 346: 462-7 and 1996; 348: 701-7).

The risk of getting malaria varies a great deal from area to area, and it also depends on when and how you travel. Travellers to Africa are at risk in most rural and many urban areas, particularly during the evening. Travellers to Asia and South America, however, often spend most of their time in towns or resorts where there is limited, if any, risk of exposure, and they travel to rural areas mainly during daylight hours when there is also limited risk of infection.

Cholera

Cholera (*Vibrio cholerae*) infection is caught from contaminated food or water and usually results from poor sanitation. In a 1991 epidemic in Peru of over 16,400 cases and 71 deaths, the epidemic was traced to drinking unboiled water, or water from a household water storage container (Lancet, 1992; 340: 28-33).

Cholera vaccination is no longer recommended for the current outbreak in South and Central America. There have been some instances in African countries where a vaccination certificate has been requested at the border, but this is not common. In any case, cholera doesn't appear to pose a serious threat to Britons, since only about 30 contract it every year, according to the Public Health Laboratory Service. Risks are higher in America, with its proximity to South America, where 10 cases were reported in just three states, following the big epidemics in South and Central America in the early 1990s (JAMA, 1991; 265: 2658-9).

Dropping the recommendations could be a tacit admission that there is no effective vaccine to date. The killed injected vaccine, which offered protection for only a few months, if at all (Ind J Biochem & Biophys, 1994; 31: 441-8), is now being replaced by a number of whole cell and live vaccines. Some studies of the killed oral WC/rBS vaccine were promising, showing a protection of 85 per cent after six months, but largely among patients with type O blood (Lancet, 1994; 344: 1273-6). A 1993 Vietnamese trial of the killed oral cholera vaccine showed an effectiveness of only 60 per cent, leading doctors to experiment with a single dose of the live oral CVD vaccine.

Nevertheless, experience demonstrated the vaccine only offers protection against certain strains (Lancet, 1997; 349: 957 and 1992; 340: 689-93). It's known, for instance, that the vaccine doesn't protect against a new strain, known as Bengal cholera, that has emerged in southern Asia.

In July 1994, in one of the worst cholera outbreaks in recent times, 12,000 Rwandan refugees died in Goma (eastern Zaire). This strain was also resistant to tetracycline and doxycycline, used to treat cholera (JAMA, 1996; 276 (5): 348). Other multiple-drug-resistant strains have emerged in Honduras (Lancet, 1997; 349: 924).

Besides fever, you can experience serious allergic reactions to this drug, nerve damage and even mental problems (Infection & Immunity, June 1996; 64 (6): 2362-4). In one study, cholera vaccine may be responsible for transverse myelitis (J Royal Society of Med, 1990; 83; 653). Other studies have shown pancreatitis (Br J Clin Pract, 1986; 40: 300-1); hepatitis B (Presse Medicale, 1986; 15: 1331); immune complex disease (Trans Royal Soc Trop Med & Hygiene, 1984; 78: 106-7); stroke (Lancet, 1985; 2: 1372); sudden death (Forensic Science Inter, 1984; 24: 95-8); myocarditis (Deutsche Med Wochenschrift, 1984; 109: 197-8); and psychiatric complications (Acta Neurological, 1974; 29: 520-33). Occasionally, side-effects are heightened when cholera has been given with typhoid vaccine (Beitrage zur Pathologie, 1976; 158: 212-24). The live (oral) form is purported to have fewer side effects (BMJ, 1993; 307: 1425).

Some data has suggested that getting cholera and yellow fever vaccines simultaneously will decrease the response of both. Although this data is disputed, Wyeth-Ayerst, who produce the injected cholera vaccine, recommends that each be given in no less than a three-week interval of the other.

Simply obeying certain hygiene rules, particularly

concerning water and uncooked food, and replacing lost fluids may protect you against all forms of cholera; studies have shown that a healthy person can have more than a billion cholera bugs in their body without developing the disease (The Times, 3 June 1993).

The most important element is to avoid the effects of severe diarrhoea, which is what eventually kills you. A patient with cholera can lose virtually twice their weight in fluid in a single day (see Alternatives, Chapter 13, for tips on rehydrating after diarrhoea).

Typhoid

Typhoid fever (caused by *Salmonella typhi*) is also spread by contaminated food and water. In Britain, some 200 people come home from holiday each year with typhoid. Typhoid vaccine is recommended for those travelling to areas where they may be exposed to contaminated food and/or water, particularly where the disease is common or sanitation particularly primitive.

The heat-phenol-inactivated injected whole cell shot has an effectiveness rate of 65 per cent but causes severe adverse reactions in one-quarter of patients (Infect Control & Hosp Epidemiology, 1991; 12: 168-72).

The typhoid vaccine should not be used in children under one year, and its harmful effects are worse in people over 35. The interaction of the fever (caused by the shots) and an underlying heart condition can cause shortness of breath, dehydration and fever (Washington Times, 23 February 1993).

Pasteur Merieux's new live Typhim VI vaccine, a polysaccharide vaccine, is purported to work better and cause fewer side effects than previously available vaccines (Military Medicine, 1990; 155: 272-4). In practice, this means an effectiveness rate of between 64 per cent and 81 per cent in countries where the disease is endemic (GP, 22 May 1992). The manufacturer warns that Typhim's effectiveness could be lowered if you have an immune disorder or are already receiving treatment that lowers your immunity. As with any vaccine, if you've already had a severe reaction to Typhim VI you should not receive it again, and it shouldn't be administered to children over six years old (Infec Con & Hosp Epid, March 1991; 12: 168-72).

Side-effects from the oral vaccine include abdominal discomfort, nausea, vomiting, fever, headache and rash. The most common side effect from the injection is redness, hardening and tenderness in the skin, which occurs in most patients. Fever, nausea, headache and flu-like symptoms have been reported in 8 per cent of patients.

People who receive the shot have fewer side-effects if it is given into the skin (intradermally), rather than under it (J of App Phys, June 1992; 72: 2322-8). Other reports of side effects include loss of consciousness, abdominal pain, vomiting, hypotension, arthralgia, kidney problems, neutropenia (lowering of blood cells) and allergic shock.

Yellow fever

This disease has plagued the tropics relentlessly. It is a viral disease transmitted to humans by mosquitoes. You may not be able to avoid vaccination if you are travelling to certain parts of Africa or South America, since you need a certificate of vaccination upon entry. The vaccine must be given at least 10 days before entering a country requiring it.

Eastern and southern African states have hitherto been free of epidemic yellow fever, hence routine vaccination is not a policy in these countries. On paper, the shot seems effective. In one study, the shot produced antibodies in 93 per cent of adults (J Biol Standards, 1986; 14: 289-95), although this fell to 60 per cent in babies (W Afr J Med, 1990; 9: 200-3).

This vaccine, which is given live, can cause encephalitis (inflammation of the brain), especially in children under nine months, although a four-year trial among pregnant women and its effect on their newborn children showed no significant side effects (Transactions of the Royal Soc of Trop Med & Hyg, 1993; 87: 337-9).

The vaccine has also been shown to cause urticaria, bursitis, neuritis, myalgia, nettle rash, inflammation tissues or nerves, jaundice, muscle pain and low-grade fever. About a quarter of patients react, and 11 per cent suffer post-vaccine syndrome of multiple pains and fever (Bul Soc Path Exotique et de Ses Fil, 1986; 79: 772-6). In one African study, a number of patients developed gangrene of the arm just a few hours after being inoculated at Shaki, Nigeria in May 1987 (Revue Roumaine de Virologie, 1994; 45: 25-30). Five went into a coma and died, although it may have been that poor hygiene or contamination was to blame.

Hepatitis A

Hepatitis A is a virus generally spread through contaminated food or water and is present in faeces. If you've travelling to places where sanitation is primitive, you need to be wary of infection. However, to put the risk of infection in perspective, of the 2,120 cases of hepatitis A contacted in the UK in 1995, 229 were presumed to be contracted abroad. It's usually seen not to be necessary unless you are visiting or planning to live in areas where the disease is highly endemic. The old shot is usually given in two stages, a year apart. You need to be inoculated at least two weeks before you travel to make sure the body has built up an immunity.

As an alternative option for a last-minute trip, gamma

globulin, a passive vaccine, injects antibodies into the system but it apparently only lasts for two to three months.

A new killed hepatitis A vaccine is now available, which is claimed to produce levels of antibodies of 88 per cent or higher, peaking within a month of administration (Vaccine, 1996; 14: 1132-6). There is some disagreement over whether a booster shot six months later is necessary, or whether you can get the booster dose two weeks after the first (J Hep, 1993; 18; Suppl 2: S32-7; Biologicals, 1996; 24: 235-42; Vaccine, 1996; 14: 501-5). Nevertheless, it does appear safer than the live injection; in a randomised controlled trial, local adverse effects were reported, with 17 per cent of those given the new vaccine, compared with two-thirds of those given the old live vaccine (Vaccine, 1996; 14: 982-6).

Nearly a fifth of recipients report malaise (Infection, 1995; 23: 334-8). and 14 per cent report flu-like syndrome and gastrointestinal tract disorders, fatigue and headache (Vaccine, 1995; 13: 220-4).

The shot was tested in a group of children in Brazil, with an outbreak of hepatitis A, and none of the vaccinated children developed symptoms or signs of hepatitis (J Med Virology, 1996; 48: 147-50). Unless you are planning to live in an endemic area, you may be able to avoid this shot by following meticulous hygiene.

Chapter thirteen

DISEASES CAUSED BY VACCINES

As well as being ineffective in giving protection against the diseases they are designed to prevent, vaccines can also create new kinds of illnesses. Being injected with a weakened or killed version of a virus can cause you to develop a viral "mutant" or encourage its growth in the population at large. Often, these previously unseen conditions can be more insidious and severe than the illness the jab was designed to prevent.

How viruses "compete" with one another

The advent of polio immunisation in 1955 caused changes in the balance of the gut viral population, favouring the spread of chronic fatigue syndrome or ME (myalgic encephalomyelitis).

No doubt polio immunisation (both the inactivated Salk vaccine and the live oral Sabin variety, introduced worldwide between 1954 and 1959) reduced circulation of the wild polio virus 1–3. However, it also altered the balance between enteroviruses, in favour of non-polio enteroviruses (NPEVs) (BMJ, 1961:1061). For instance, in 1959, polio caused 84 per cent of enterovirus associated paralysis; by 1961, its incidence had fallen to 12 per cent. But after 1961, other enteroviruses such as old and new varieties of coxsackievirus caused 74 per cent of all enterovirus-associated paralytic disease. Between 1959 and 1965, the Nightingale Research

Foundation concludes there may have been a changeover from polio as the prevalent disease to ME and other diseases caused by enteroviruses.

A similar changeover followed the introduction of oral polio vaccine (OPV) in China since 1971. The prior incidence of polio fell, while cases of Guillain-Barre Syndrome (GBS), another paralytic disease, rose sharply (Lancet, 8 October 1994).

These produce a much greater variety of symptoms, since the NPEVs are more widely distributed in the body than is polio (muscle, joints, heart, endocrine and lymphoid organs), according to ME specialist Dr Elizabeth Dowsett. Otherwise, lesions in brain stem, mid and hind brain and upper spinal cord are identical in polio and ME, according to 150 post mortems done in 1948 on US Army veterans with a history of polio (JAMA, 1947; 134: 1148-54).

In viral populations, the polio virus can easily be displaced by echo or coxsackieviruses, and this second enterovirus may be more virulent than the polio virus it replaces (Lancet, 1962: 548-51). Post-1955 ME patients have been frequently shown to have severe muscle failure (BM Hyde, *The Clinical and Scientific Basis of ME/CFS*, 1992:111-6).

Many gut viruses other than polio virus 1-3 can cause paralytic polio and ME. This is because they can attach to more than one set of tissue receptors found on different cells in the brain, spine and other body areas, as can polio. Injury to such cells results in ME symptoms, which also occur in polio and post-polio syndromes.

The presence of these non-polio gut bugs also appears to alter responses in the population to the various vaccine strains of polio. During a 1955 polio epidemic in areas of Iceland that had been exposed to the 1948-49 outbreak of epidemic neuromyasthenia (the early name for ME), children had a lower antibody response to polio vaccine strain but an increased response to polio vaccine strains 2 and 3 (Lancet, 1958; *i*: 370-71). Later, it was discovered that other viruses can inhibit the pathological effects of classic polio (IRSC J Int Res Coms [Med Sc], 1974; 2: 22-26).

Enteroviruses easily mutate—hence the polio strain used in vaccines "wanders". There have been countless reports of vaccine failure, polio contracted by fully vaccinated populations and parents contracting polio from vaccinated infants. In these, the weakened, supposedly safe vaccine strain of polio has transformed into a virulent enterovirus—either one of the classic polio ones or a strange mutation of it. Over 64 epidemic outbreaks of ME have been published in the past 70 years, two-thirds after the introduction of polio immunisation 40 years ago (Am Jnl Med, 1959: 569-95; AM Ramsay, *Myalgic Encephalomyelitis and Postviral Fatigue Syndromes*, Gower Med Publ, 1988; SAMJ, 1988; 74: 448-52; Postgrad Med J, 1988; 64: 559-67).

In epidemic form, this disease strikes teaching and medical establishments (ME is more common in teachers than in health care workers). The earliest epidemic outbreaks usually occurred in the wake of a polio epidemic, the first at LA County General Hospital in 1934 (Publ Health Bulletin 240, Washington DC, 1938), referred to as "atypical polio". Another, which affected officers and men in Switzerland in 1939, was described as "abortive poliomyelitis" (Helvetica Med Acta, 1949; 16: 170-72), as was a 1950 NY State outbreak (Neurology, 1954; 4: 506-16).

Hib and other meningitis strains

Eradicating one strain of a virus can also encourage other forms of it to proliferate. This is precisely what's happening with the Hib meningitis vaccine. As b-type *H influenzae* strains are being wiped out by vaccination, mutant non-b *H influenzae* strains are thriving.

A study in The Lancet (1993; 341: 851-4) examined 408 strains of Hib meningitis. Although 94 per cent were *H influenzae* type b, the rest were non-serotypable *Haemophilus influenzae* (NST) strains. The Lancet story concluded that vaccination will have no effect on the incidence of infection of these mutant strains: "Infections due to these *H influenzae* strains are, after the implementation of Hib vaccines, likely to persist and represent a substantial proportion of the serious infections caused by this species," it said.

An accompanying editorial said that Hib meningitis comprises only 40–60 per cent of all invasive Hib infection. "As more Hib vaccine is used, the greater, proportionally, will be the role of non-capsular *H influenzae* that are a major cause of acute otitis media (middle ear infection) sinusitis, exacerbation of chronic bronchitis and other mostly respiratory infections," wrote writer Heikki Peltola.

A similar situation occurred with US army recruits being tested with a killed adenovirus pneumonia vaccine in the 1960s. According to Harold S Ginsberg (*The Adenoviruses*, New York: Plenum Press), the vaccine caused unpredictable shifts in the virus type. Epidemics of disease from these mutant viruses occurred among recruits, rendering the vaccine useless and sending the scientists scurrying back to the laboratory to try to develop a vaccine that would knock out the mutations as well.

How vaccines can cause ME

ME is a provocation disease. That is, a range of co-factors— a virus, a viral and a bacterial infection, stress, surgery, vaccination, inherited allergies and toxic chemicals—can make someone susceptible to the virus that seems to cause

ME (Loria, RM, *Coxsackie \viruses: A General Update*, Plenum, 1988).

Vaccines are themselves an onslaught on the immune system. When you are vaccinated, your immune system is otherwise engaged; and during this window of vulnerability other infections (such as viral ones) can lead to ME—a latent infection turns into an acute attack or relapses from earlier infections can occur. We know, for instance, that cell-mediated immunity—that is, your immune system response in your cells—is depressed for up to six weeks after measles vaccination (*ABPI Data Sheet Compendium 1994/5*).

According to Sir Graham S Wilson, Honorary Lecturer at the Department of Bacteriology, London School of Hygiene and Tropical Medicine, many different types of vaccine can precipitate polio in a child who was earlier vaccinated with the live polio virus (GS Wilson, *The Hazards of Immunization*, 1967: 265-80).

Muscle damage caused by the needle can allow the polio virus already present in the body following previous vaccination to track up the nerves. This occurred in Russia, where children are commonly given injections of antibiotics. This provoked polio strains from vaccines to spread from the damaged muscle to the spinal cord, causing paralytic polio.

The weakened live viruses in vaccines can themselves mutate, causing new disease in the population. A group of researchers found that one so-called wild circulating enterovirus most closely resembled the polio vaccine virus (Brit Med Bull, 1991; 47:4; 793-808). ME patients have also been found to be infected with mutant or defective viruses (J Gen Virol, 1990; 71: 1399-402).

Polio and ME

A body of clinical evidence linking ME to polio is growing.

The proceedings of the first international scientific conference on the post-polio syndrome in the US have been collated in the Annals of the New York Academy of Science. It includes 50 papers written by 118 contributors from a wide range of specialities, including clinical neurology, neuroscience, electrophysiology, brain imaging, histology, virology, immunology, epidemiology and rehabilitation.

In particular, papers by Dr Richard Bruno, assistant professor at the New Jersey Medical School's Department of Physical Medicine and Rehabilitation, and director of Post-Polio Rehabilitation and Research Service at the Kessler Institute for Rehabilitation in New Jersey, and four other specialists compare in graphic detail ME—now often called Chronic Fatigue Syndrome—and post-polio syndrome (Dalakas, et al, ed. *The Post Polio Syndrome: Advances in the Pathogenesis and Treatment, Annals*, NY Academy, Sciences, 1995: 273: 1-409).

Post-polio is developing in those who had polio 25-30 years previously. Clinically, it is indistinguishable from ME. Other researchers demonstrate that ME is just another form of polio, which has increased with the advent of polio vaccination. As one type of gut virus has been eradicated, so other forms have had the space to proliferate.

There are several angles from which to investigate the theory that ME is a type of polio. One is its clinical symptoms. Dr Elizabeth Dowsett, consultant microbiologist of the Southeast Essex NHS Trust who is in the forefront of ME research, explains that true ME (as opposed to fatigue states with other aetiologies) appears clinically as being polio-like, and it has often been diagnosed as a "non-paralytic polio."

"These patients have weakness, pain down their spines and are systemically ill," she says.

She feels that it has been an unfortunate mistake to turn to the label "chronic fatigue" because true ME is a neurological condition that usually originates with a gut virus infection like coxsackievirus. Apart from clinical examination, in some cases of ME you can actually demonstrate the presence of gut-virus infection in the patient. The requirement to put off diagnosing ME for six months after the patient falls ill has unwittingly prevented this.

If tests are not done very rapidly after the onset of infection, it is too late to identify the virus. A blood screening test called the IGM, which shows up recent infection, is an NHS procedure. This can be positive up to three months after infection in adults. As the enteroviruses are characterised by their relapsing nature (on average, three-week intervals), it could also be identified on relapse.

Apart from modern techniques, a research procedure called the acid elution test can remove antibodies from a circulating virus and can be applied to viruses multiplying in the bowel. Years ago it was difficult to diagnose polio, and it was this very test which was used.

A third way to compare ME with polio is by looking at studies of actual outbreaks which identified the viruses causing it. Here the evidence is particularly striking.

A paper by Richard T Johnson, at the Department of Neurology, John Hopkins University School of Medicine, in Baltimore, Maryland, published in the 1995 Annals of the New York Academy of Sciences, sets out evidence that has been available since the 1950s. "In the spring of 1957," he wrote, "we investigated an epidemic of poliomyelitis in Hawaii. . . of the 39 cases of non-paralytic poliomyelitis, only four were related to type 1 polio virus. There were 16 cases of echo virus 9, seven cases of coxsackie, and four to five other enteroviruses."

The very enteroviruses known to be implicated in so-called

ME were here identified as causing non-paralytic polio. ME has often been diagnosed as non-paralytic polio. And even more interestingly, two of the 38 cases of paralytic disease were not caused by the polio virus at all, but by one of the coxsackieviruses.

So we know that enteroviruses in general can cause varying forms of the disease we call polio. Other parallels between ME and polio concern neurological damage.

In the November 1991 edition of Orthopedics, Dr Bruno says: "All the evidence available shows conclusively that every case of poliomyelitis, human or experimental, exhibits lesions of the brain. In the experimental animal this included non-paralytic and abortive cases as well as paralytic cases."

Abnormalities can now be demonstrated in the brains of people with ME using SPECT and MRI scans. You would expect there to be differences in the diseases caused by different viruses, but if these viruses are all of the same family and use the same receptor sites in the body, you would also expect there to be similarities. This is just what we find.

Dr Bruno says: "Despite the differences between poliomyelitis and ME, an association with the polio virus was suggested by the fact that, of the more than one dozen ME outbreaks before the introduction of the Salk vaccine, nine occurred during or immediately after outbreaks of polio, and several involved hospital staff who cared for polio patients" (Annals, NY Academy of Sciences, 1995). There is also the case of a woman who fell ill with classical ME/CFS while nursing a friend with acute paralytic polio (Hyde et al, *Epidemiological Aspects of ME/CFS*, Ottawa: Nightingale Research Foundation, Canada, 1994).

But if ME is a type of polio, why doesn't everyone exposed to the relevant viruses develop ME just as they did polio? It has been forgotten that, as Dr Thomas Stuttaford of The

Times explains: ". . .only a small number of those infected with the polio virus became paralysed; about 90 per cent didn't even realise that they had anything more threatening than a cold." With polio and ME, the state of your immune system governs whether you will be susceptible. By altering the population's resistance to a particular organism, we alter the balance of infectious agents in the environment. The circulation of wild polio viruses 1–3 may have declined through vaccination. However, this has left us open to the other 69 polio-related viruses, which have thrived. It is therefore not surprising that since the late 1950s the incidence of ME has risen, and experts predict that it will be the neurological disease of the 21st century. By suppressing the spread of three enteroviruses we have opened the door to the rest.

The argument about whether enterovirus infection persists over many years is still raging. In her 1995 review of the proceedings of the 1994 Post-Polio Conference, Dr Dowsett draws attention to new evidence of persistent enterovirus infection in the central nervous system of post-polio patients.

She concluded: "Three separate groups of virologists from the USA, UK and France have found fragments of enteroviral RNA in the spinal cord, cerebrospinal fluid and blood of some patients with Post-Polio syndrome. The fragments are identified as polio virus by some and as coxsackievirus by others."

It is thought that the emergence of late-onset post-polio fatigue may result from age-related changes in brain cells that survived the original polio infection (Bruno, Annals, NY Academy of Sciences 1995). But it can be observed through case histories that just as we see post-polio syndrome 30 years after initial infection, so we are seeing "post-ME" as well.

The Nightingale Research Foundation in Ottawa proposes

that in fact they are one and the same condition—others believe they may be variations of each other.

The researchers concluded that what has arisen is "two new diseases with different names, with different degrees of acceptance and exactly the same set of symptoms at exactly the same time. It is unrealistic to believe that we are dealing with two different disease processes and two different causes."

A paper investigating the epidemiological aspects of ME/CFS has revealed further convincing parallels between the behaviour of this disease and polio. It describes the onset of ME as mainly being ushered in by a "minor illness" which has "recently been described as a flu-like illness. . .". The researchers continue: ". . .in reality it is identical to and has all of the features and variability of the minor illness of missed or abortive poliomyelitis".

In comparisons with epidemic polio going back to 1916, they note that "we see the same two typical features" in a typical year with an epidemic of ME: "a decreasing incidence from January to reach a summer low; then. . . the strong late summer increased incidence, peaking in the August to October period" (Hyde et al, *Epidemiological Aspects of ME/CFS*). ME, or atypical polio, is a serious and devastatingly debilitating multi-system malfunction leading to such profound weakness in some children that they are unable to speak and have to be tube-fed. But they can breathe; enteroviruses have an affinity for certain tissues and many do not attack the respiratory centre causing its paralysis, as in polio itself.

Atypical measles
Soon after the measles vaccine was first developed and universally administered, a new and serious problem began

to come to light: vaccinated children were contracting what became known in the medical literature as atypical measles, an especially vicious form of measles resisting treatment.

A 1965 study in Cincinnati described nine cases which occurred there two years earlier during an epidemic of measles (Am J Dis Child, 1965; 109: 232-7). According to Viera Scheibner (*Vaccination*), the authors followed 386 children who had received three doses of killed measles virus vaccine in 1961. Of these 386, 125 had been exposed to measles and 54 had developed the disease. "It is obvious that three injections of killed vaccine had not protected a large percentage of children against measles when exposed within a period of two-and-a-half years after immunisation," wrote authors L W Rauh and R Schmidt. Many of these children were so ill with high fever and pneumonia that they had to be hospitalised.

Two years later, according to Scheibner, a study described the occurrence of atypical measles in 10 children who had received the inactivated (killed) measles virus vaccine five to six years earlier. Nine children developed pneumonia which resisted all treatment (J Am Med Ass, 1967; 202: 1075-80). Serious reactions also occurred in children originally injected with killed measles virus, and then re-vaccinated with live measles virus (N Engl J Med, 1967; 277 (5): 248-51).

Another illness sparked by the measles vaccine, says Scheibner, was so-called "mild measles" with under-developed rash, which exposes children in later life to dangers of chronic diseases, including cancer. One study found evidence of a relationship between lack of rash in measles and increased incidence of degenerative and auto immune diseases (Lancet, 1985; *i*: 1-5). Furthermore, many practitioners say that cancer patients have a particularly small number of infectious diseases of childhood to report in their medical history.

Autism

The London firm of solicitors which represents many children allegedly damaged by the measles, mumps and rubella vaccine—Hodge, Jones and Allen—says that a good half of all the MMR cases they are bringing involve children who were developing normally but then became autistic right after vaccination.

Of those reporting problems, 123 have reported autism— twice as many as any other problem. Although, in general, 350 cases of autism are reported every year, suggesting that there should be 5,600 cases among children from one to 16, some 10,000 cases have been reported in one British county alone.

According to a conference paper by Dr Sudhir Gupta at the University of California's Department of Medicine, a study of autistic patients shows the "strong association between immunisation with MMR and the development of autism (regressive autism)". (See also J Autism, Development Disorders, 1996; 26 (4).) (See Chapter 5.)

Crohn's disease and diabetes

The measles vaccine may trigger the bowel conditions ulcerative colitis and Crohn's disease in adults. Researchers at London's Royal Free Hospital have found that vaccinated people were three times as likely to go on to develop one of these conditions, as were those who caught measles naturally. Vaccinated people were also 2.5 times more likely to develop ulcerative colitis.

Their findings were based on a study comparing 3,500

people who had the vaccine in 1964, with 11,000 people born in 1958 who were not vaccinated (Lancet, 29 April 1995).

The late medical critic Dr Robert Mendelsohn maintained that the many long-term side-effects of the live measles vaccine include multiple sclerosis, juvenile onset diabetes and Reye's syndrome. Reye's syndrome can cause the degeneration of organs such as the pancreas, particularly when aspirin has been used. Mendelsohn once cited a batch of cases of Reye's syndrome in Montreal in which five of the children had been vaccinated within three weeks of coming down with the illness. In *A Shot in the Dark*, Harris Coulter also provides ample evidence of the relationship between pertussis vaccination and the failure of children to maintain stable glucose levels.

One **WDDTY** reader believes that her daughter Jennifer's diabetes was brought on by the measles vaccine. Jennifer was vaccinated against measles when she was a year old. After the injection she suffered various side-effects for a few days, including chesty cough, runny nose and general "unwellness".

"For the following four-and-a-half years," her mother writes, "Jennifer had problems with her left arm at the site of the injection. There were lumps under the skin and obvious discomfort and irritation, which caused her to scratch the area continually, often resulting in bleeding. Then about six months ago, the problems with the skin at the injection site disappeared.

"At the same time, Jennifer started to exhibit symptoms of not being 100 per cent well. She was easily tired, quite lethargic and subject to quite violent mood swings. She became more and more uncooperative in her general behaviour. She also started to drink a lot of fluids and lose weight. She was eventually diagnosed as diabetic. I was devastated. There is no history of diabetes in our immediate family. I am faced with the prospect of injecting her with insulin at least once a day for the rest of her life."

Polio and cancer

There may well be a link between contaminated polio vaccines, given routinely three or four decades ago, and rare cancers. Between 1955 and 1963 large batches of polio vaccine were inadvertently contaminated with a monkey virus called simian virus 40 (SV40), which was found to cause cancer in laboratory animals.

Scientists thought then that there was no risk to humans. But recently, researchers have discovered evidence of SV40 in tissue samples from people stricken with rare childhood brain tumours, as well as bone and abdominal cancers (JAMA, 1997; 277: 873). This new evidence was recently considered by 250 scientists at the National Institutes of Health in the US where it was concluded that we could not rule out the role which SV40 may have played.

Hepatitis B and arthritis

The hepatitis B vaccine has been linked with cases of arthritis. In a recently reported case, two health workers given the vaccine suffered attacks of arthritis. One contracted Reiter's Syndrome, a form of arthritis, believed to be the first linked to the vaccine.

The cases, at the UK's Leicester Royal Infirmary, join a growing number of similar cases reported since the Engerix B vaccine was introduced into Britain in 1987, reports Dr Wajahat Hassan at the Infirmary. In all, 3.2m doses have been given, especially to those at higher risk of infection from handling blood, such as healthcare workers (BMJ, 9 July 1994).

Whooping cough and asthma

The whooping cough vaccine may be to blame for the rise in the number of children developing asthma. During a study into the protective effects of long-term breastfeeding, Dr Michael Odent, of the London-based Primal Health Research Centre, came up with a surprise finding—children immunised against whooping cough were six times more likely to have asthma than those who hadn't been given the jab (J Amer Med Assoc, 1994; 272: 592-3). In virtually every category—number of sick days, cases of earache, admittance to hospital—the unvaccinated children were healthier.

Chapter fourteen

ALTERNATIVES TO VACCINATION

The subject of childhood vaccinations makes emotions rise fast. Some people believe it is everyone's social duty to have their children vaccinated, others feel angry that they were bullied into it by doctors without knowing all the facts, while others refuse point-blank to have their children inoculated because of the dangers and risks they see associated with the vaccines.

Those in this last group usually also believe in alternative remedies and good nutrition to build up their children's own immune system to fight off disease. We spoke to some of these to find out what alternatives they use in place of vaccinations.

Kelly Holden, a medical herbalist who runs the Holden Natural Health Clinic, in Ashstead, Surrey, is totally against vaccinations and uses herbal formulas for herself and her children. Many of her clients are mothers and she tries to encourage them to do the same.

The Holdens are a family of vegans; a healthy diet helps build the immune system, she believes. She doesn't use an alternative to vaccinations as such, but uses two types of herbal formulas as an anti-infection tincture and an immune-boosting tincture, which she also uses when they go abroad. She would never go to a country where vaccinations are mandatory. Her immune-boosting formula includes tinctures of the following: boneset; echinacea; Siberian ginseng; pau d'arco; prickly ash; thuja; and wild indigo. Her anti-infection tincture comprises: cayenne; echinacea; garlic; golden seal; myrrh; poke root; plantain; self heal; and tea tree oil.

Garlic, she says, is the best antibiotic, antiviral, antibacterial, antifungal ("in fact, anti-everything, except anti-life!") plant to be found. She claims that the drug companies have done more research into garlic than into any other herb, and it is well known that garlic destroys cancer tumours.

"But the drugs companies have obviously kept this quiet for fear that they will lose money on their own so-called remedies if this becomes public knowledge," she says.

Mrs Helen Knipe buys only organic food for her and her family. She says eating healthily will build up the immune system. Unfortunately, due to lack of support in hospital, she didn't breastfeed her twins. She now boosts them up with evening primrose and fish oils.

Laura Hanlon's four-year-old has had the DPT jab, but not MMR. Her 11-month-old hasn't had any jabs yet. Ms Hanlon believes in good nutrition to help build the immune system, and so is very conscious about what they eat. But she also goes to a professional homoeopath and would rely on him for alternatives if necessary. For example, she would consult him if she was going abroad where vaccinations are recommended.

Susan Godsland has refused most of the vaccines, and relies on good health and nutrition. With most of the milder illnesses, she's glad if her children catch it when they're young, as this builds up their immune system for later on in life.

Kim Day hasn't had her children vaccinated for anything except tetanus, a necessary protection, she feels, as they live next to a farm. She breastfed both her children for 19 months to give their immune systems the necessary right start. Her own diet, therefore, had to be good. She takes supplements and both her children take chewable vitamins and mineral supplements now. She also ensured that she was in good health before getting pregnant; she believes pre-conceptual care is a great help.

She goes to a homoeopath, but he has never suggested an alternative to vaccinations, although he says there are antibodies. She does worry about her children picking something up from, say, a public swimming pool, and would bathe them in lavender oil afterwards, which is antibacterial and antiviral. She's also heard that blueberries are very good against the polio virus.

She added that her own father had polio when he was four years old, and the doctors said he would never walk again. But his mother massaged his legs and took him swimming in the sea every day for a year (even when it was cold). After a year of this, he could stand again. He was then encouraged to roller skate to build up his muscles. His legs are perfectly normal now.

Mary Caunter has been visiting alternative practitioner Jack Temple, a dowser and healer, for six years. Mr Temple recently made the national newspaper headlines because he has been treating members of the Royal Family.

Mr Temple applies a particularly powerful herb (which he found on the Isle of Skye) in homoeopathic form, which he places above the elbow, in the bone marrow area.

He also uses this herb on pregnant mothers, once he's "cleaned" them up generally. For example, a lot of women have nylon in the body when they visit him, so he has to rid them of this before treatment can begin, as it is poisonous. He insists that they wear only natural fibres.

He is a believer in pre-conceptual care, so likes to see them before they become pregnant.

Terry Moule, president of the British Naturopathic Society, who speaks regularly about alternatives to vaccinations, suggests that if you aren't going to vaccinate, make sure to stimulate your child's immune system properly. This includes breastfeeding for as long as possible (and eating an organic wholefood diet since pesticides and other chemicals tend to accumulate in breast tissue). Once you introduce solids, make sure that your child is getting a balance diet of organic food rich in selenium, zinc, vitamin C, vitamin E and potassium. If you have doubts that his levels of these vitamins are adequate, do have him take high quality supplements.

Steer your child away from processed food, food with colouring and additives, and an excess of white flour. Terry Moule also believes that we should not allow our children to be overly sanitised; exposure to mild bacteria in your child's environment also stimulates the immune system.

Because of worries about security and the temptation of sedentary activity like computer games, today's children get far less exercise than earlier generations. Make sure your child gets regular exercise and fresh air—both shown in studies to help boost immune function.

Another immune booster is cold showers after baths, which stimulate skin function—important in both immune function and elimination of toxins. Although other vaccine critics like Peter Mansfield believe it is important to keep your children close to home when they are tiny, to avoid their exposure to too many foreign germs, Moule believes that exposing your child to others is another way to strengthen his immune function.

Finally, if your child does contract an illness like whooping cough, many homoeopaths claim to be able to successfully treat it.

Vitamin A for measles and polio

When vitamin A levels are low, the outer layer of our mucous membranes become scaly and the turnover of cells decreases. The measles virus infects and damages these tissues throughout the body. Blood concentrations of vitamin A, even in the well nourished child, may decrease to levels normally associated with malnourished children. Giving vitamin A to childen with measles can lessen the complications or chances of dying from the disease (New Eng J of Med, 1990; 323: 160-4).

Indeed, Gerald Keusch of Boston's New England Medical Center, which conducted this study among pre-school children in India, went on to say that vitamin A ought to be administered to children whenever there is evidence of a vitamin A deficiency or a possibility of complications from measles.

In the Mvumi Hospital in central Tanzania, 180 children admitted with measles were randomly given routine treatment alone or additional, large doses of vitamin A (200,000 IU orally immediately on admission and again the next day). Of the 88 children given vitamin A, six died; of the 92 not given the supplement, twice as many (12) died. The difference in mortality was most obvious for children under two; death rates were reduced by seven times among those given vitamin A (BMJ, 1987; 294: 294-6).

During measles, children with marginal liver stores of vitamin A may develop an acute vitamin A deficiency, resulting in eye damage and possibly increased deaths from respiratory diseases and diarrhoea. One other study showed that even children with only a mild vitamin A deficiency were more at risk (Lancet, 1986; i: 1169-1173). Another study documented an increased risk of respiratory disease and diarrhoea in children with pre-existing mild vitamin A deficiency (Am J of Clin Nutr, 1984, 40: 1090-5).

Measles, coupled with acute vitamin A deficiency, can lead to the eye condition xerophthalmia—which causes dryness and inflammation of the transparent membrane lining the eyelids and the lower eyeball—in many developing countries. In 1992, New York researchers measured vitamin A levels in 89 children younger than two years with measles against a control group. Among the children with measles, 22 per cent had lower vitamin A levels. Those with lower levels of vitamin A were more likely to have fever of 40°C or higher, to have fever for seven days or more and to be hospitalised. They also had lower measles-specific antibody levels (Am J Dis Child, 1992; 146: 182-6).

If your child has had measles or a measles jab, you can request that his blood antibody levels be checked before subjecting him to risks of the shot. If you decide not to go ahead with the jab, you can boost your child's immunity by feeding him a varied wholefood diet rich in vitamin A, good sources for which are carrots, liver, butter, green leafy vegetables, egg yolks and cod liver oil.

If you do decide to use vitamin A supplements, it's safer to use beta carotene (a precursor to vitamin A) since excessive levels of vitamin A can be toxic. Vitamin A supplements should only be taken under supervision. Make sure you consult a qualified, experienced nutritionist for advice about appropriate levels. The NutriCentre in London advises the following daily doses of beta carotene:

Age	Dosage
1-3	2,000 international units (IUs)
4-5	2,500 IUs
5-12	5,000 IUs
·12-17	15,000 IUs

For more advice, please contact The NutriCentre on 0171 436 5122.

Vitamin A is also reputed to offer protection against polio-type viruses (**WDDTY**, 1996; 7 (2): 8).

Cholera

Following strict hygiene rules, particularly concerning water and uncooked food, and replacing lost fluids may protect you against all forms of cholera; studies have shown that a healthy person can have more than a billion cholera bugs in his body without developing the disease (The Times, 3 June 1993). It is vital to avoid the potentially fatal dehydrating effects of severe diarrhoea by replacing lost fluids.

Malaria

There is one exciting development for malaria treatment on the horizon: a plant called qinghao (known as wormwood or *Artemisia annua* in the West). This herb, which has been used in Chinese medicine for thousands of years to treat a variety of ailments, has been recognised as an anti-malarial drug in China since the early 1970s.

The Chinese have demonstrated that it is more rapidly acting than any other antimalarial, with no evident toxicity (Lancet, 1993; 341: 603-8; Trans R Soc Trop Med Hyg, 1994; 88 (Suppl I): S9-S11).

In some parts of South-Eastern Asia (particularly the eastern and western borders of Thailand)—where the failure rates of treatment with high-dose mefloquine alone in falciparum malaria now exceed 40 per cent—artesunate taken orally with mefloquine over three to five days still remains highly effective (Lancet, 1992; 339: 821-4; J Infect Dis, 1994; 171: 971-7).

According to two separate studies, artemisia was found to

be as effective as quinine in preventing deaths from severe malaria (New Eng J of Med, 1996; 335: 124-6). These herbs also seem to be faster-acting than other anti-malarials and there appears to be no evident toxicity, although individual responses may vary, as with all herbs (Lancet, 1992; 339: 649-50).

Other natural possibilities are extracts of cinchona bark, the natural source of quinine, which have been used in South America for centuries to treat malaria-type fevers (New Eng J Med, 1992; 327: 1519-21).

If you can get hold of an experienced Chinese herbalist, it might be prudent to take this herb, which has a better track record than most of the drugs on the market. However, its not registered and therefore not generally available in many countries. The British vitamin company Biocare produces it as a general anti-parasitic (Tel: 0121-433 3727).

Homoeopathic nosodes

Nosodes—the homoeopathic equivalent of vaccines—are available which are designed to protect against most of the childhood diseases traditionally vaccinated against. Nosodes can also be considered if you're travelling to countries where vaccination has been recommended.

Some 52 years before Koch first isolated the tubercle bacillus for the tuberculosis vaccine, nosodes (homoeopathic dilutions of the products of the illness in question, given orally) were commonly used as just-in-case measures against a wide variety of diseases.

According to government statistics, the use of homoeopathic vaccines was accompanied by an amazing drop in the incidence of whooping cough, diphtheria, scarlet fever and measles in children. In all groups, the numbers of people of all ages contracting TB, dysentery, typhoid fever and Asiatic cholera plummeted (Gaier, *Thorsons Encyclopaedic Dict of Hom*, HarperCollins, 1991).

The few published studies to have looked at this area suggest that nosodes are effective at preventing specific diseases (Alternatives, **WDDTY**, February 1995; 5 (11): 9).

In one large-scale study, more than 18,000 children were successfully protected against meningitis with a homoeopathic remedy (Meningococcinum IICH) with no side-effects (FX Eizayaga, *Treatis on Homoeopathic Medicine*, Buenos Aires: Ediciones Marcel, 1991).

Nevertheless, there is much disagreement among homoeopaths about whether nosodes are effective or even necessary. Many feel that a healthy immune system— supported by diet and homoeopathy—will protect a child better than homoeopathic "vaccines".

Before deciding to use homoeopathic nosodes, you should consider how great the risk is of contracting a particular disease. As with conventional vaccinations, there is no point in having a treatment unless you are at risk of contracting the condition in the first place.

Besides nosodes, the homoeopathic pharmacy Helios offers the following prophylactic remedies for travellers (one dose— ie, one pill—only unless otherwise stated). Again, there is fierce disagreement over whether taking the traditional treatments for a disease will help to ward it off:

Cholera
One Camphor 30 at bedtime and one on rising to be taken two weeks before travelling to an infected country.

Hepatitis
One Chelidonium 30 to be taken eight days before departure; and repeat the dose once every week of your stay.

Polio
One Lathyns satirus 30 to be taken seven days before departure.

Malaria
One Natrum mur 30 to be taken six days before departure; and repeat the dose once every week of your stay.

Yellow Fever
One Arsenicum album 30 to be taken five days before departure.

Typhoid
One Manganum 30 to be taken three days before departure.

Meningitis
If meningitis becomes epidemic while you're away, take one Belladonna 30 weekly.

Tetanus
If you get a cut or puncture wound, take Ledum 30.

Cholera, hepatitis A and B, and typhoid
In areas with poor sanitation and hygiene, you should assume that beer, wine, canned or bottled carbonated drinks, and beverages made with boiled water are the only safe drinks. To ensure that empty bottles were not refilled at the local tap and recapped, even bottled water you drink should be carbonated (though be aware that some brands may be high in sodium).

Always avoid ice cubes, and remember that alcohol will not make mixed drinks made with plain tap water safe. Consider non-disposable glasses and cups unsafe, too; so skip formalities and drink from the original drink containers using sanitary straws.

Boil your own safe water supply for hygienic purposes such as brushing your teeth, washing near your mouth, and so on. Boil water vigorously one minute for each 1,000 feet (300 metres) above sea level. You may want to take an inexpensive immersion coil along for boiling.

If bottled carbonated water is not available and boiling is not practical, your best alternative is to treat water with either iodine additives or tetracycline hydroperiodide tablets. Remember to filter cloudy water through a clean cloth or coffee filter to remove sediment before treating.

Food presents risks as well. You should avoid leafy and uncooked vegetables and salads. Fruits, nuts, and vegetables can be safe if they are well cleaned and have an intact thick skin or shell, which you should peel yourself, taking care not to contaminate the inside.

Order meats, fish and other seafood cooked well done and served piping hot. Bread is safest when served fresh from the oven. Avoid moist grain dishes (like rice) that have been allowed to sit at room temperature for prolonged periods.

Always avoid cold meat platters, mayonnaise and creamy desserts, as well as buffets and street vendors. Always refuse unpasteurised dairy products, including cheese and yoghurt. To protect against any attempts by local sellers to stretch pasteurised milk by adding water or unpasteurised milk to cartons or bottles, stick to canned milk.

Don't swim or fish in polluted waters, and don't eat fish that may have been caught in such waters.

When you are out and about, try to keep your hands away from your face. Always wash your hands when you return, and always wash your hands before eating.

Japanese encephalitis, yellow fever and malaria

Every traveller's first line of defence is to take personal protective measures against mosquitoes, even if you choose to be vaccinated. There is still a risk of contracting other mosquito-borne illnesses in Asia. The mosquitoes which transmit Japanese encephalitis feed mainly outdoors during the cooler hours at dusk and dawn. You should avoid being outdoors during these times and wear mosquito repellent. If it contains DEET, a 30 per cent concentration is generally adequate. Stay in air-conditioned or well-screened rooms.

Also reduce your amount of skin exposure by wearing socks, long trousers and long-sleeved shirts. If you use a repellent containing DEET on children, do so with care because of the potential for neurological side-effects associated with overdoses.

If you will be travelling in rural areas, carry along a portable bed net, and aerosol room insecticides to kill indoor mosquitoes. You can apply permethrin (a mosquito repellent/insecticide) to clothing and mosquito netting.

Nets are a highly effective means of cutting risk of malaria. The number of deaths from malaria among African five year olds has been cut by up to a third and hospital admissions have plummeted by 40 per cent through the use of bed and door nets impregnated with the biodegradable insecticide pyrethroid. WHO estimates after large-scale trials the lives of half-a-million children could be saved each year simply by using the nets. The other bonus is that nets reduce the frequency of severe infections and allow immunity to develop naturally for children in the area (BMJ, 1996; 312: 995).

Ultimately though, your best protection against disease comes from looking after your health generally and taking simple, common-sense preventative measures, like avoiding taking young children and babies to known danger areas.

Don't eat raw fish, or such things as ceviche, a South American dish made with raw fish. One study in Trujillo, Peru suggests that raw seafood played a minor part in a cholera epidemic (Lancet, 1992; 340: 20).

Some vegetables, such as cabbage, are irrigated with raw wastewater in arid parts of the world such as Peru (Lancet, 1992; 340: 20).

Chapter fifteen

YOUR LEGAL RIGHTS

Just 11 hours after baby Rose was born, two police officers, two social workers and three ambulance men arrived to take her away from her parents. Their crime? Refusing to have Rose vaccinated against hepatitis B immediately after she was born.

Mother, father and baby were subsequently taken to hospital to await a court order directing that the baby be vaccinated. Neither parent had been able to attend the court hearing to put their side of the story. Not surprisingly, after months of harassment by the authorities, the mother had a nervous breakdown.

This is an extreme and, we hope, unrepresentative case of what can happen to families who don't toe the line over vaccination. Rose's mother was known to be a carrier of hepatitis B and so her baby was deemed to be at particular risk of contracting this potentially fatal disease. The most parents who refuse to have their children vaccinated can usually expect is a lecture each time they see their doctor or, at worst, being struck off his list.

However, this story may be an object lesson in the lengths the authorities can go to if they feel they are being challenged head on.

Like most parents who resist vaccination, Rose's parents were not recklessly putting their child's health at risk but acting in what they—and a number of experts they contacted—believed were in her best interests. Their objections to the jab were two-fold: they didn't accept the vaccine was effective and feared it would compromise their baby's immune system; and they were concerned about its side-effects. They had good reason for the latter concern, given that their first-born child had suffered severe dermatitis for nearly a year after being given a hepatitis B booster jab.

None of this, however, cut any ice with the medics or the courts, who were determined to bully Rose's parents into submission. The authorities threatened to take Rose away from them permanently if they continued their resistance, and Rose's father was even threatened with a manslaughter charge should she die in later life from hepatitis. Even when they had been browbeaten into agreeing, Rose was still made a ward of court to ensure she received two booster shots (Mothers Know Best, August 1995; 1 (3); 1-2).

Despite what happened to baby Rose, parents have the absolute legal right to refuse all vaccinations for their children. The authorities in her case could resort to the law to force vaccination because of the special circumstances involved—but this is not generally an option. However, this doesn't stop many doctors resorting to emotional blackmail or other kinds of pressure, such as threatening to strike off recalcitrant families. Although your doctor may honestly believe you are putting your child's health at risk by refusing vaccination, you should be aware that there may also be a financial motive. Vaccination pays for your GP's holiday. He receives a fee only if a large percentage of his patients get vaccinated (see Introduction, page 7).

Although anecdotal evidence suggests that some GP practices routinely strike off those who refuse vaccination, they are not entitled to do so. One mother whose GP had such a "jab-or-jump" policy wrote to the Health Secretary (then Virginia Bottomley) to complain. Mrs Bottomley wrote to the GP and forced him to re-instate the family as patients.

What the law says

On the face of it, the law is fairly clear about where rights and responsibilities lie when it comes to children. Section 1, subsection 1 of the Children Act 1989, states that the children's interest are paramount. The law can only intervene if it feels the actions—or inaction—of parents are threatening the well-being of the child, a point that has been tested in common law as well.

Normally, a parent's consent has to be given before any treatment can start if the child is deemed to be too young to fully understand the arguments. This right is not, however, absolute, and the courts can intervene if treatment is considered to be in the best interests of the child—as happened with baby Rose.

If the doctors or authorities in a case are vehemently opposed to a parent's decision, they can ask the courts to intervene. The court will be asked to determine what is in the child's "best interest"—based on the evidence presented to it. If treatment is to be given without parental consent, the principle of necessity has also to be established. In practice, this involves an emergency medical procedure when the child's life is at risk.

Two important precedents were established in law in 1993 by the Jehovah's Witnesses, who are opposed to blood transfusions. The first established that only the High Court could decide whether a transfusion should take place in the face of parental objection; the second established that in any procedure which did not involve a life-threatening situation, alternative measures should be offered.

These decisions would be likely to set a precedent in any

other situation that was not life-threatening: "More and more of our cases are not coming to court because there are alternatives to blood transfusions," a Jehovah's Witnesses spokesman said. "Courts often feel that the parents are in the best position to decide."

Meanwhile, Rose's parents are continuing their fight on the basis that the authorities' actions were illegal.

What you can do

If you've read all the arguments for and against vaccination and have firmly decided against (and we urge you to become highly informed before making that choice), here are a few suggestions to ensure that your child isn't vaccinated against your wishes:

Never allow anyone else to take a young child to any doctor or hospital. One child we know of accompanied his au pair on her visit to the GP. While she was being tended to, a nurse, who recognised the boy, whisked him off and gave him the MMR jab, much against his parents' wishes. If your child goes to hospital for any reason, make sure you indicate in writing that you do not wish him to have any vaccines. Hospital is a favourite place for unauthorised, "catch-up" vaccines.

During school vaccination campaigns, make sure you sign and return the consent form, clearly stating that you do not want your child vaccinated. During this last campaign, unreturned forms were taken to be a "yes". Or even better, keep your child at home that day—to avoid having him jabbed inadvertently.

Experience suggests that—when the vaccination of your own children is the issue—discretion is the better part of valour. If at all possible, you should try to avoid getting into a head-to-head confrontation with any doctor or organisation (such as a school) who wants you to have your child vaccinated. We have found that however well informed you are and however convinced of your case, you will almost always signally fail to derail a pro-vaccination zealot.

By entering into an argument and drawing attention to your "maverick" decision, you will simply prompt attempts to try to change your mind. We know of many parents who refused to agree to vaccination during a recent measles campaign by writing "we have made an informed choice" (or something similar) on the consent form. They were subsequently badgered by letters, phone calls and the like from officials arguing the case with them.

Other parents, however, have found that they are left in peace if they write instead: "We have been advised against vaccination for medical reasons." (Of course, the "medical reasons" are the numerous studies showing questionable safety and effectiveness.) This information will go into your child's school file, and possibly travel with him to other schools—which should ensure he is left alone. It may be wise to write in similar terms on the entry form for your child's nursery, primary and secondary schools in case the situation ever arises where he would be given a jab.

Try to avoid arguing about vaccination with your doctor. There are numerous ways you can try to head off a direct confrontation. Tell him that you haven't decided yet whether to have your child vaccinated; you are seeking a second opinion; you will have the jabs later; or that you wish to have them done privately; that your child hasn't been well; or any other good excuse. Confronting him directly invites him to attempt to use coercion. Luckily, the authorities probably couldn't legally enforce vaccination unless there were special circumstances—as with baby Rose. But this case does show that some doctors and officials are prepared to use whatever weapons are available to them to bully reluctant parents.

As we discussed above, striking off individuals or even whole families appears to be a favourite tactic. If this happens to you, you should write to the Secretary of Health to complain and ask that he intervene to have you reinstated (if, of course, you still want to put your family's health in the hands of a doctor who took such a high-handed attitude).

Suing for damages

Suing for compensation if you suspect your child has been damaged by a vaccine is fraught with difficulties. Many cases have failed because of the difficulty of proving to the courts that it was the jab that caused the problem. With the pertussis vaccine, for example, the High Court ruled in 1988 in the case of Moira Lovejoy that there wasn't enough evidence to prove the vaccine could cause brain damage. However, UK lawyers have taken heart from the Kenneth Best case, a landmark decision in the Irish Supreme Court. The court overturned an earlier ruling and awarded damages of 2.75m against the drug manufacturer Wellcome for vaccine damage.

In the light of the Best judgement, solicitors are hopeful that they may be able to establish a link for many other vaccine victims. Payments of up to 30,000 have already been paid—albeit with no admission of liability—under the British government's vaccine damage scheme. Thus far, legal aid has been granted in some 80 cases for neurological assessments of brain damage.

To have any hope of bringing a successful case, you will need to amass as much evidence as possible. Keep a record of dates of vaccinations, date of the onset of problems, batch numbers, and the content of any discussion with doctors that may be relevant—such as if you warned them that your child had a history of reacting badly to jabs but they insisted you go ahead, anyway. You should also be sure to see a firm of solicitors experienced in this complicated field of law. See list of contacts for organisations that can help you (page 173).

Consent form

The following, prepared by a lawyer, is our suggested alternative consent form for any vaccine. Ask your doctor, the nurse administering the jabs, or even your local health authority in charge of implementing the programme to sign this form. In effect, it is asking the Department of Health to put its money where its mouth is.

This consent form may also be used as a means of preventing the health authorities from pestering you if you have decided against vaccination (some parents who have said "no" have been telephoned or sent new consent forms to "reconsider" by health workers).

Our guess is that most doctors and nurses will run a mile from our consent form. Feel free to photocopy this and circulate it among other interested parties.

For information about how to avoid compulsory vaccination in the US (see Contacts, page 173).

Vaccine Consent Form

Child's Name:

I give my consent for my child to be vaccinated with the vaccine(s) subject to the following conditions:

1. That the information which has been supplied is fully accurate both as to the safety and the efficacy of the vaccine.

2. That the doctor or nurse performing the vaccine, the Health Authority, the manufacturer of the vaccine and the Department of Health will accept full joint and several responsibility for any injury caused to my child as a result of the vaccine being administered.

3. That, in the event of any such injury being caused, my child will receive full compensation, assessed in accordance with the normal principles of English Tort Law.

If these conditions are not acceptable, the vaccination should not take place.

Date:

Signed:

Prepared by What Doctors Don't Tell You, 4 Wallace Road, London N1 2PG

Chapter sixteen

FURTHER READING
AND CONTACTS

Books

A Shot in the Dark, by **Harris Coulter** and **Barbara Loe Fisher** ($10.00 plus $1 for postage to the Center for Empirical Medicine, 4221 45th Street, NW, Washington, DC 20016).
The seminal work on the dangers of the DPT vaccine.

Vaccination, Social Violence and Criminality, by **Harris Coulter**.
A fascinating discussion of the relationship between mass vaccination and the rise of learning disabilities, hyperactivity, autism, and criminality ($15 plus $1.50 postage at the same address as above).

Vaccination and Immunisation: Danger, Delusions and Alternatives, by **Leon Chaitow** (CW Daniel Co, Essex, 1987).

Vaccination, by **Dr Viera Scheibner** (178 Govetts Leap Road, Blackheath, NSW 2785, Australia. Aus$30).
An excellent summary of the medical research into vaccines and their effects.

Vaccinations: The Rest of the Story, by **Mothering Magazine**.
A Selection of Articles, Letters and Resources 1979-1992. All

the articles the magazine has run about vaccination, now in book form ($14.95 plus postage to same address as above).

Vaccines: Are they Really Safe and Effective?, by **Neil Z Miller** ($6.95 from Vaccine Booklet, New Atlantean Press, PO Box 9638, Santa Fe, NM 87504).

The Dangers of Immunization, Vaccinations and the Immune Malfunction, and How to Legally Avoid Unwanted Immunizations of All Kinds, ($9 for the set from **The Humanitarian Publishing Company**, RD3 Clymer Road, Quakertown, PA 18951).

What Every Parent Should Know About Childhood Immunization by **Jamie Murphy** (Earth Healing Products, PO Box 11, Dennis, Massachusetts 62628. $13.95).

The Vaccine Guide: Making an Informed Choice by **Randall Newstaeder** (North Atlantic Books, PO Box 12327, Bakeley, CA 94712. $14.95)

Contacts
The National Health Federation
(212 W Foothill Blvd, PO Box 688, Monrovia, CA 91016 USA). Mainly for Americans living in areas requiring immunisation. Send $6 plus postage for their Immunisation Kit which provides information about how to avoid compulsory immunisations, and which states offer exemptions.

Dissatisfied Parents Together (DPT)
128 Branch Road, Vienna VA 22180 (Tel: 703-938-DPT3). Has information about compensation for damage following vaccination.

The Informed Parent
PO Box 870, Harrow, Middlesex HA3 7UW (Tel: 0181 861 1022).

JABS
1 Gawsworth Road, Golborne, Warrington, WA3 3RF (Tel: 01942 713565).